Communications in Computer and Information Science　1311

More information about this series at http://www.springer.com/series/7899

Jiangtao Wang · Longbiao Chen ·
Lei Tang · Yunji Liang (Eds.)

Green, Pervasive, and Cloud Computing – GPC 2020 Workshops

15th International Conference, GPC 2020
Xi'an, China, November 13–15, 2020
Proceedings

Editors
Jiangtao Wang
Coventry University
Coventry, UK

Longbiao Chen
Xiamen University
Xiamen, China

Lei Tang
Chang'an University
Xi'an, China

Yunji Liang
Northwestern Polytechnical University
Xi'an, China

ISSN 1865-0929 ISSN 1865-0937 (electronic)
Communications in Computer and Information Science
ISBN 978-981-33-4531-7 ISBN 978-981-33-4532-4 (eBook)
https://doi.org/10.1007/978-981-33-4532-4

This Springer imprint is published by the registered company Springer Nature Singapore Pte Ltd.
The registered company address is: 152 Beach Road, #21-01/04 Gateway East, Singapore 189721, Singapore

Preface

On behalf of the Organizing Committee, we are pleased to present the adjunct proceedings of the International Conference on Green, Pervasive and Cloud Computing (GPC 2020), held in Xi'an, China, on November 13, 2020. The adjunct workshops aim to establish a high-standard world forum for researchers and practitioners alike to share their novel ideas and experiences in the areas of urban computing, intelligent transportation, and social computing.

Although the COVID-19 pandemic has triggered the most widespread global economic meltdown and incredible academic hardship, the adjunct workshops provide a great opportunity to share the ongoing research works and to learn from the emerging solutions in the fields of Internet of Things and pervasive computing. In total, we received 16 submissions. Each submission received at least three reviews. Among them 4 submissions were accepted as full papers and 4 submissions were accepted as short papers. The overall acceptance rate is 50%.

We really appreciate the contributors who made the adjunct workshops happen. First and foremost, The Chinese government went to great effort to cease the widespread of COVID-19 within its borders, which made it possible to host the adjunct workshops in China. Second, we greatly appreciate the authors who submitted and presented their contributions during the workshops. Third, we appreciate the Program Committee members and reviewers who dedicated their time to the advancement of knowledge. Without their hard work and guidance, the conference simply would not have happened.

We hope you enjoy the adjunct proceedings.

November 2020

Lei Tang
Yunji Liang
Jiangtao Wang
Longbiao Chen

Organization

Organizers

Jiangtao Wang	Coventry University, UK
Lei Tang	Chang'an University, China
Yunji Liang	Northwestern Polytechnical University, China
Longbiao Chen	Xiamen University, China
Zhiyong Yu	Fuzhou University, China
Hongkai Yu	Cleveland State University, USA
Rui Ma	The University of Alabama in Huntsville, USA

Program Committee

Ying Li	Chang'an University, China
Xiaoyan Yin	Northwest University, China
Na Fan	Chang'an University, China
Yishui Zhu	Chang'an University, China
Jianwu Fang	Chang'an University, China
Xiao Lin	GAC R&D Center Silicon Valley, USA
Yun Yang	Chang'an University, China
Junchi Ma	Chang'an University, China
Chao Chen	Chongqing University, China
Dingqi Yang	University of Fribourg, Switzerland
Leye Wang	Peking University, China
Sha Zhao	Zhejiang University, China
Thi-Mai-Trang Nguyen	Sorbonne University, France
Xiaolong Zheng	Institute of Automation, Chinese Academy of Sciences, China
Xuan wei	The University of Arizona, USA
Sagar Samtani	University of South Florida, USA
Helei Cui	Northwestern Polytechnical University, China

Contents

Urban Computing

Differential Private Spatial Decomposition for Mobile Crowdsensing Using Staircase Mechanism

Qi Liu, Jianmin Han$^{(\boxtimes)}$, Xin Yao, Juan Yu, Jianfeng Lu, and Hao Peng

College of Mathematics and Computer Science, Zhejiang Normal University,
Jinhua 321004, China
hanjm@zjnu.cn

Abstract. Although mobile crowdsensing (MCS) has become a new paradigm of collecting, analyzing, and exploiting massive amounts of sensory data, sharing the sensory data with users' sensitive location data may expose them to potential privacy. Differential privacy is a popular privacy preservation approach, which could realize strong privacy protection in various scenarios, ranging from data collection, data releasing, to data analysis. In this paper, we focus on the noise adding mechanism in constructing differentially private spatial decomposition. The noise adding mechanism, as the standard approach to preserving differential privacy, directly affects the utility of differentially private data. To improve the accuracy of counting query on the private two-dimensional spatial datasets, we propose a Staircase mechanism based differentially private Uniform grid partition method, namely Staircase_Ugrid. We first investigate the relationship between non-uniform error and query intersection area, and utilize the linear least square to fit the linear relation between them. Then we deduce the optimal partition granularity by minimizing non-uniform error and noise error. In the experiments, we use two real world datasets to evaluate the performance of the proposed method. Experiments show that the proposed two-dimensional spatial publishing method makes a good trade-off between data privacy and utility.

Keywords: Mobile crowdsensing · Differential privacy · Staircase mechanism · Spatial data

1 Introduction

The proliferation of smart phones and wireless network enable the collection of large amount of location data during our daily lives. These location data generated by mobile phone users is valuable for crowdsensing applications, such as urban planning, human mobility and intelligent transportation systems, to name a few. However, the collection and release of location data could cause privacy issues [23]. Therefore, there have been quite a lot of researchers work on the problem of privacy protection in location data release.

© Springer Nature Singapore Pte Ltd. 2020
J. Wang et al. (Eds.): GPC 2020 Workshops, CCIS 1311, pp. 3–17, 2020.
https://doi.org/10.1007/978-981-33-4532-4_1

Differential privacy [1, 2] is a rigorous privacy model, and provides provable privacy guarantees. In this paper, we work on the problem of releasing differentially private synopsis for two-dimensional location data, which has been investigated in [3]. In particular, given a location dataset and the space domain (two-dimension) of the dataset involved. We firstly divide the space into cells with grid partition; then generate noisy counts for each cell in a way that satisfies differential privacy; finally release the boundaries of these cells and their noisy counts as the differentially private synopsis of the given dataset. The released synopsis can be used either for generating a synthetic dataset, or for answering queries directly [3].

Several researchers have attempted to develop methods of releasing differentially private synopsis for two-dimensional datasets [4–6], [3]. Xiao et al. [4] considered the problem of differentially private histogram release, and proposed two-multidimensional partitioning strategies, i.e., the grid partition and the KD-tree-partition. Cormode et al. [5] focused on constructing differentially private spatial indices, such as quad-trees and KD-trees, to provide a private description of the data distribution. The emphasis of private spatial indices is on how to perform the partitioning. Qardaji and Li [6] proposed a general recursive partitioning framework for multidimensional datasets. At each level of recursion, partitioning is performed along the dimension, which results in the most balanced partitioning of the data points. The balanced partitioning employed by this method has the effect of producing regions of similar size. When applied to two-dimensional datasets, this approach is very similar to building a KD-tree based on noisy median. Qardaji et al. [3] concentrated on grid partition of two-dimensional datasets, and exanimated the relationship between the two sources of error (i.e., noise error and non-uniform error) and the grid size. They proposed a method for choosing the optimal grid size for the uniform grid partition, and proposed an effective parameters determination method for adaptive grid partition.

Most existing works on the release of differentially private location statistics focused on the problem of space decomposition method, whereas the noise adding mechanism to the statistics of each divided regions is seldom considered. In this paper, we focus on the problem of the optimal noise adding mechanism to generate location synopsis, which reserve same level of differential privacy with lesser amount of noise addition, as the utility of differentially private synopsis is closely related to the noise-adding mechanisms. To achieve this goal, we propose a Staircase mechanism based on differentially private Uniform grid partition of two-dimensional space, namely Staircase_Ugrid. The staircase mechanism [7], which is a geometric mixture of uniform random variables, can replace the Laplace mechanism with the same level of differential privacy. The main contributions of this paper are as follows.

- Investigate the relationship between the non-uniform errors and intersection areas with query range, and propose new method for adaptively fitting the parameter of the relation model.
- Adopt the Staircase mechanism to randomize the statistics of each grid cell, thereby reducing the amount of noise error.
- Experiments on two real world datasets demonstrate the effectiveness of the proposed method, which makes significant improvements in terms of query accuracy and efficiency.

2 Related Works

In this section, we review the state-of-the-art works of preserving privacy while releasing users' location and recent noise-addition mechanism of differential privacy.

Generally, there are four main classes of privacy protection: secure multi-party computation (SMC), homomorphic encryption, k-anonymity, and perturbation. The first class, SMC solutions [16, 17], allows a group of mutually distrustful parties to compute a joint function on their inputs without revealing any information beyond the result of the computation. This will incur a high communication or computation overhead when participant population is large. The second class [18, 19] allows any third party to operate on the encrypted data without decrypting it in advance. However, to interpret the final aggregation, a third party needs to know which users reported data, which is not always desirable. The third class, anonymity-based approaches [20, 21], generalize quasi identifiers, ensure that an individuals' data is indistinguishable from at least (k−1) others. Unfortunately, these methods have been fund to be vulnerable to many types of privacy attack, such as foreground knowledge attack [22]. The fourth class [8] makes no assumption about user's background knowledge and quantifies the level of privacy protection. It becomes one of the most promising privacy models in privacy-preserving data mining.

Currently, Laplace mechanism is the standard method of adding noise to data. Dwork et al. [8] proposed a Gaussian mechanism to add Gaussian-distributed noise to the query results in the process of data releasing so as to make it satisfy (ε, δ)-differential privacy. Consider the accuracy of publishing results, sensitive data publishing work with adjustable privacy protection budget that satisfy differential privacy have been proposed one after another. Koufogiannis [9] proposed an adjustable Laplace mechanism, which gradually adjusts the privacy budget and adds Laplacian noise with markov property to achieve differential privacy. Since Laplace mechanism only satisfies ε-differential privacy, Du Xiajie [10] proposed an adjustable Gaussian mechanism, which is more universal.

3 Problem Definition

3.1 Differential Privacy

Definition 1. Differential privacy [11]: A randomized mechanism M satisfies ε-differential privacy if for any pair of neighboring datasets D and D', and any $S_M \in Range(M)$,

$$\Pr[M(D) \in S_M] \leq exp(\varepsilon) \times \Pr[M(D') \in S_M] \tag{1}$$

ε is the privacy budget and $exp(\varepsilon)$ is the probability ratio of algorithm M to output the same value on two neighboring datasets, which reflects the level of privacy protection provided by algorithm M. The smaller the privacy budget, the higher the degree of privacy protection.

Differential privacy is achieved by adding an appropriate amount of noise to the returned value of the query. Adding too much noise will reduce the utility of the results, and too little will not provide enough privacy protection. Therefore, how to determine an optimal amount of noise is the key to differential privacy. To this end, the researchers defined the sensitivity to determine the amount of noise added.

Definition 2. Sensitivity [1]: For a given function $f : D \rightarrow R^d$, its sensitivity is

$$\Delta f = \max_{D,D'} \|f(D) - f(D')\| \tag{2}$$

for all D and D', differing in one record. Sensitivity is a parameter that controls the amount of noise added to query results, and reflects the largest impact of change one record in the data set on the query results.

Based on the fundamental concept above, the technique for achieving differential privacy is introduced as follows.

Definition 3. Staircase Mechanism [7]: For a multidimensional real-value query function $q : D \rightarrow R^d$ with sensitivity Δ, the Staircase mechanism will output

$$K(D) = q(D) + Staircase(\Delta, \varepsilon, \gamma)^d \tag{3}$$

where $Staircase(\Delta, \varepsilon, \gamma)$ is a random variable with probability density function

$$f_\gamma(X) = \begin{cases} e^{-k\varepsilon}a(\gamma) & \|X\|_1 \in [k\Delta f, (k+\gamma)\Delta) \\ e^{-(k+1)\varepsilon}a(\gamma) & \|X\|_1 \in [(k+\gamma)\Delta f, (k+1)\Delta) \end{cases} \tag{4}$$

All Staircase random variables are independent.

Definition 4. Sequential Composition [12]: Suppose that each algorithm Ag_i provide ε_i-differential privacy. A sequence of Ag_i over a database D provides $\sum \varepsilon_i$-differential privacy as a whole.

Definition 5. Parallel Composition [12]: Suppose that each algorithm Ag_i provides ε-differential privacy. A sequence of Ag_i over a set of disjoint data sets D_i provides ε-differential privacy as a whole.

3.2 Error Model

In the release of location statistics, the granularity of partition restricts the accuracy of statistical query, and the number of partitioned blocks determines the amount of noise. Both of them determine the utility of statistic in the release. Therefore, the error of the released results mainly comes from the noise error and the non-uniform error.

(1) Noise error

In order to prevent an attacker from inferring the user's true position from a large number of query results, the releasing will use a noise-enhancing mechanism that satisfies

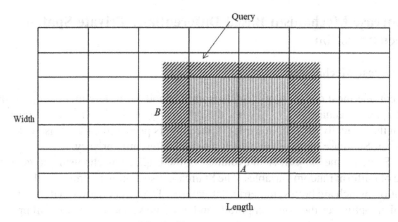

Fig. 1. Two types of error

differential privacy to add noise. The effect of adding noise on query result is called noise error

$$e_{noise}(D) = \left| \tilde{Q}(D) - Q(D) \right| \tag{5}$$

Where D is the partitioned areas, $Q(D)$ and $\tilde{Q}(D)$ are original statistics and noise statistics of the partitioned areas. If the granularity of partition is large, there will be a large number of null nodes where the count is 0. Because the privacy budget is given, the section of privacy budget allocated to each empty node is small, thus introducing a large amount of noise error and reducing the usefulness of the released statistics.

(2) Non-uniform error

The data distribution in a certain area is always assumed to be uniform since the two-dimensional area partition cannot be accurate to a single point. At this time, the range count query algorithm calculates the query result according to the ratio where the query intersects with the area, and the intersecting part is shown as the diagonal line in Fig. 1. Non-uniform error is the range count query error caused by the use of uniform hypothesis estimation:

$$e_{non-uniformity} = \left| \sum\nolimits_{i=1}^{m} r_i \cdot Q(d_i) - Q(D) \right| \tag{6}$$

where $d_i(i = 1, 2 \cdots, m)$ denotes the partitioned blocks that intersect with rectangle query. $r_i(i = 1, \cdots, m)$ denotes the ratio of query area in the block. This type of error depends on the distribution and grouping of points in the dataset. In the intersected area between rectangle query and partitioned blocks, the size of the non-uniform error generally depends on the number of data points in the blocks. Therefore, the finer the granularity of the partition, the smaller the non-uniform error.

4 Staircase Mechanism Based Differentially Private Spatial Decomposition

4.1 Staircase Mechanism

At present, the most common noise-enhancing method for differential data publishing is the Laplace mechanism [3, 13], but the optimality of the Laplace mechanism has not been theoretically proven. In work [7], the authors proposed a new noise-enhancing mechanism-Staircase mechanism, which satisfies differential privacy.

The Staircase mechanism is an evolution of the Laplace mechanism and geometric mixture of uniform random variables. The Staircase distribution is similar to the Laplace distribution, which are both symmetrical structures. The theory shows that the Staircase mechanism optimizes the noise amplitude and noise power, so less noise will produced under the same privacy budget.

To minimize the expectation of the amplitude of noise, the optimal noise probability distribution has probability density function with

$$\gamma^* = \frac{1}{1 + e^{\frac{\varepsilon}{2}}} \tag{7}$$

and the minimum expectation of noise amplitude is

$$\Delta \frac{e^{\frac{\varepsilon}{2}}}{e^{\varepsilon} - 1} \tag{8}$$

the optimal noise probability distribution has $\gamma^* = -\frac{b}{1-b} + \frac{(b - 2b^2 + 2b^4 - b^5)^{\frac{1}{3}}}{2^{\frac{1}{3}}(1-b)^2}$, where $b = e^{-\varepsilon}$, and the minimum expectation of noise power is

$$\Delta^2 \frac{2^{-2/3} b^{2/3} (1 + b)^{2/3} + b}{(1 - b)^2} \tag{9}$$

We generate random variables with Laplace distribution and Staircase distribution according work [7, 14], and the histograms are shown in Fig. 2. Taking the privacy budget as 0.4 as an example, the corresponding Staircase distribution variable is more concentrated around 0, that is, a smaller random variable is generated with a larger probability, which shows that the Staircase mechanism make less perturbation on numerical output under the same degree of privacy protection. We introduces the Staircase mechanism into the two-dimensional space partition for the first time in order to improve the accuracy of published data.

4.2 Spatial Decomposition Model

At present, the most common idea for two-dimensional space partition is uniform partition, which partitions the spatial area into grids with the same size, and then obtains the noisy value of each grid. However, the query accuracy is highly dependent on the grid size. As for the selection of grid size, the idea of existing work [3, 13] is to obtain

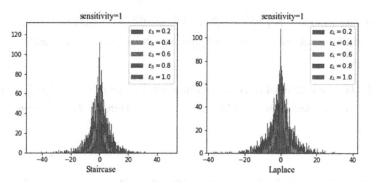

Fig. 2. Noise histogram

the optimal solution of partition granularity by minimizing two kinds of errors. In this paper, we use the analysis ideas in work [13] to quantify noise error and non-uniformity error.

(1) Noise error

As the sensitivity of count query is 1, the noise added for each cell follows the distribution Staircase($1, \varepsilon, \gamma$) and has a deviation of $\frac{2^{-2/3}b^{2/3}(1+b)^{2/3}+b}{(1-b)^2}$. Given a $m \times m$ grid, and a query that selects r portion of the domain (where $r = \frac{AB}{LH}$, the ratio of the area of the query rectangle to the area of the whole domain), about $\frac{AB}{LH} \cdot m^2$ cells are included in the query, and the total noise error has deviation $\frac{2^{-2/3}b^{2/3}(1+b)^{2/3}+b}{(1-b)^2} \cdot \frac{m^2AB}{LH}$. We set $S = \frac{2^{-2/3}b^{2/3}(1+b)^{2/3}+b}{(1-b)^2}$, so the noise error is $e_{noise} = m\sqrt{Sr}$.

(2) Non-uniformity error

As illustrated in Fig. 1, let cells that are filled with oblique lines be α. We have the following observations:

• The non-uniformity error is proportional to the number of data points in the cells that are filled with oblique lines.
• The non-uniformity error is 0 when α is 0.

Motivated by the observations above, we propose that the relation between non-uniformity error β and α is $\beta = k\alpha$. k is the proportionality coefficient, which can be calculated by least square estimation:

$$k = \sum (\alpha_i - \bar{\alpha})(\beta_i - \bar{\beta}) / \sum (\alpha_i - \bar{\alpha})^2 \tag{10}$$

(α_i, β_i) is the ith sampling value; $\bar{\alpha}$ and $\bar{\beta}$ are the mean value of non-uniformity β and α. The number of cells that intersected with the border of Query is $\frac{2Am}{L} + \frac{2Bm}{H}$, and the area of each cell is $\frac{LH}{m^2}$, so we can deduce that the total area of the cells that intersected with the border of Query is $\left(\frac{2Am}{L} + \frac{2Bm}{H}\right) \cdot \frac{LH}{m^2} = \frac{2AH+2BL}{m}$. According to the relation between non-uniformity error β and α we proposed above, we have non-uniformity error $e_{non-uniformity} = k \cdot \frac{2AH+2BL}{m}$.

Lemma 1. The total error of query is at a minimum when $m = \left\lceil \sqrt{\frac{4kHL}{\sqrt{s}}} \right\rceil$, where k is the proportionality coefficient, H and L are the width and length of the domain of dataset D.

Proof:
The total error of query is the sum of non-uniformity error $e_{non-uniformity}$ and noise error e_{noise}, where $e_{non-uniformity} = k\frac{2AH+2BL}{m} \geq \frac{2k\sqrt{4AH \times BL}}{m} = \frac{4k\sqrt{HL} \times \sqrt{rHL}}{m} = \frac{4kHL\sqrt{r}}{m}$, $e_{noise} = m\sqrt{sr}$.

To minimize the total error $e_{non-uniformity} + e_{noise}$, we deduce that $m = \sqrt{\frac{4kHL}{\sqrt{s}}}$, and round it up to a smallest integer. Then, $m = \left\lceil \sqrt{\frac{4kHL}{\sqrt{s}}} \right\rceil$.

4.3 Algorithm

In order to further balance the impact of noise error and non-uniform error on the publication of two-dimensional data partition, a Staircase_Ugrid method based on Staircase mechanism is proposed in this paper. This method first divides the location space into independent cells based on the optimal partition granularity. Then traverse the data set to count the number of points in each cell. Finally, by adding noise with Staircase distribution on each cell count, combined with the parallel combination theorem of the differential privacy algorithm, the differential data privacy of the published data is generally realized.

The pseudo-code description of the Staircase_Ugrid algorithm is shown in Algorithm 1. First of all, Staircase_Ugrid calculates the optimal partition granularity of the two-dimensional region based on the given parameters; Steps 2–6 of Staircase_Ugrid conduct domain division in spatial dataset D; step 7 obtains the true point count of each divided cell; Step 8 to 9 add noise with Staircase distribution to the true count of each divided cell; Finally, the two-dimensional spatial statistics are published that satisfy the differential privacy.

Algorithm 1: Staircase_Ugrid

Input: spatial dataset D, privacy budget ε, sensitivity Δ

Output: sanitized $\tilde{D} = \{\tilde{d}_1, \tilde{d}_2, ..., \tilde{d}_i, ..., \tilde{d}_{m \times m}\}$

1. Calculate the optimal partition granularity $m = \left\lceil \sqrt{\frac{4kHL}{\sqrt{s}}} \right\rceil$

2. for $(i=1; i \leq |D|; i++)$ do

3.   if $(point_i \in c_i)$ then

4.   Add $point_i$ to cell c_i

5.   end if

6. end for

7. Set point count $d_i = |c_i|$

8. for $(i = 1; i \leq m \times m; i++)$ do

9.   noisy count $\tilde{d}_i = d_i + Staircase(\varepsilon, \Delta, \gamma)$

10. end for

11. return sanitized dataset d $\tilde{D} = \{\tilde{d}_1, \tilde{d}_2, ..., \tilde{d}_i, ..., \tilde{d}_{m \times m}\}$

4.4 Privacy and Time Complexity Analysis

Theorem 1. Algorithm Staircase_Ugrid satifies ε-differential privacy.

Proof. The process of adding noise with Staircase($\varepsilon, \Delta, \gamma$) distribution to the count of each independent cell satisfies ε-differential privacy. According to the parallel combination theorem of differential privacy, Staircase_Ugrid satifies max(ε_i)-differential privacy. As $\varepsilon_i = \varepsilon$, Staircase_Ugrid satifies ε-differential privacy.

Theorem 2. Given spatial dataset D and the optimal partition granularity m, the time complexity of Staircase_Ugird is $O(|D| + m^2)$.

Proof. In steps 2–6 of algorithm 2, dataset D has $|D|$ data points, and the cost is $|D|$. In steps 8–10, there are m^2 cells, and the cost is m^2. Therefore, the total cost of the Staircase_Ugird is $O(|D| + m^2)$.

5 Experimental Evaluation

5.1 Experiment Setup

Datasets

We illustrate the datasets by plotting the data points directly in Fig. 3. We also present the parameters for these datasets in Table 1.

The first dataset named storage includes US storage facility locations. There are about 9000 data points. We choose this dataset to analyze whether our analysis holds for both large and small datasets.

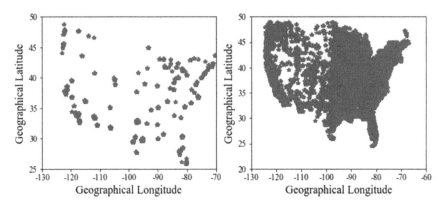

Fig. 3. The visualization of two datasets

Table 1. Experimental information about datasets

Parameter	Dataset	
	Storage	Landmark
Number of points	8938	870052
Domain size	55 * 25	60 * 26
Size of q_1	1.250 * 0.625	1.250 * 0.625
Size of q_2	2.500 * 1.250	2.500 * 1.250
Size of q_3	5.000 * 2.500	5.000 * 2.500
Size of q_4	10.000 * 5.000	10.000 * 5.000
Size of q_5	20.000 * 10.000	20.000 * 10.000
Size of q_6	40.000 * 20.000	40.000 * 20.000

The second dataset named landmark is obtained from infochimps, including about 870 k data points. The landmark dataset consists of locations of landmarks in the 48 continental states in the United State.

Competitors and Implementation Details
In this section, we compare and analyze the Staircase_Ugrid, Lap_Ugrid [13], UG [3], AG [3], and Qopt [15] algorithms from two aspects of the utility and efficiency.

The experimental environment is: i5-4200 M processor, 8G memory, Windows 10 operating system, Python 3.6.2.

It has been shown that the two types of query error will reach the maximum around the medium size in related work [3, 13, 15]. So q_1, .., q_6 query covers about half of the query area as far as possible. We set six kinds of rectangular queries in the experiment. The privacy budgets were set to 0.1, 0.5, and 1.0. We randomly generated 600 queries in each rectangular query, and the average value was used as the experimental result. The data set and rectangle query specific information are shown in Table 1.

5.2 Evaluation Metrics

Relative error and absolute error are adopted to estimate the utility of sanitized data. The relative error is defined as:

$$\text{RE}(Q) = \frac{|Q(D) - Q(\tilde{D})|}{max\{Q(D), |D| * 0.1\%\}} \tag{11}$$

where $Q(D)$ denotes the real query result, $Q(\tilde{D})$ denotes the noisy query result, $|D|$ is the total number of data points in D. And the divisor is $|D| * 0.1\%$ when $|D| = 0$, which avoids dividing by zero.

5.3 Experimental Results

5.3.1 Parameter Learning

As shown in Fig. 4, we take the storage dataset as an example and plot the fitting of intersected area and non-uniformity by linear least squares fitting, which verifies the rationality of the previous assumptions. Proportionality coefficient in Fig. 4 is 0.58, we can deduce that $\beta = 0.58\alpha$. It is easy to see that non-uniformity error will increase as intersected area increase.

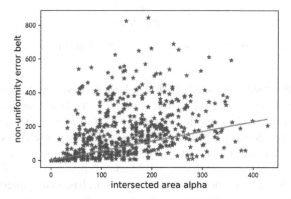

Fig. 4. The effect of fitting

5.3.2 Utility

In order to verify the robustness of the proposed partitioning method, experiments were performed on two datasets with different sample sizes and data skewness. The privacy budget is set to 0.1, 0.5, and 1.0, respectively. At the same time, in order to verify the validity of the experimental results, the experiment both show the relative error and absolute error.

Figure 5 shows the relative error of range query of the Staircase_Ugrid, UG, Lap_Ugrid, AG, Qopt on different datasets. The relative error on landmark dataset is smaller than storage's, which can be contributed to different distribution of dataset, the landmark dataset is with a uniform location distribution while the storage dataset is with a sparse location distribution. We can observe that the error is large when the query is in mid-size. Because many blank areas exist in the dataset, the corresponding true data count is very small, and a lot of noise is added to meet the differential privacy protection, resulting in large query errors. We can also find that increase the privacy budget will decrease the relative error on all datasets.

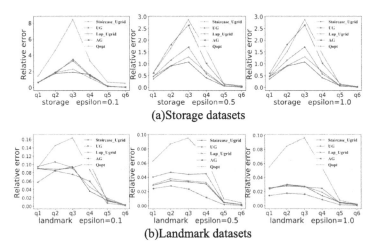

Fig. 5. Relative error of range query under different privacy budget

The experiment results show AG performs best, followed by Staircase_Ugrid that proposed in this paper, and Qopt performs worst. The Staircase mechanism is an improved form of the Laplace mechanism, and performs better when the privacy protection requirement is low [7]. The Lap_Ugrid has a slightly worse effect than the Staircase_Ugrid algorithm since the privacy budgets we set here are small $(0.1, 0.5, 1.0)$. The AG algorithm performs better due to the good trade-off between non-uniform error and noise error by two-stage partition. The Qopt algorithm has a large query error since it is independent of the data distribution and the depth of the tree is difficult to determine. It is noted that the performance of the AG algorithm is poor on the storage dataset, which may be related to the sparseness of the dataset and the privacy budget allocation of the algorithm. In work [3], the author did not theoretically derive the optimal privacy budget allocation strategy, but only distributed the privacy budget evenly, which would have an impact on the query results.

Figure 6 shows the absolute error of range query of the Staircase_Ugrid, UG, Lap_Ugrid, AG, Qopt on different datasets by candlestick. The candlestick provides five data node, and sorts the absolute error in a descending order: are the upper edge (maximum), upper quartile, median, lower quartile, and lower edge (minimum). We can know the distribution of absolute error through candlestick.

It can be seen from Fig. 6 that the overall distribution of the absolute error corresponding to the AG algorithm is low, followed by Staircase_Ugrid and Lap_Ugrid, and

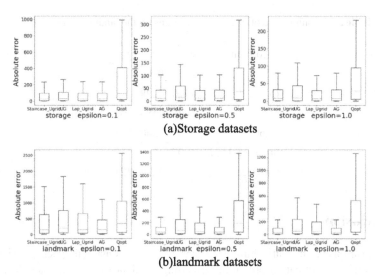

(a)Storage datasets

(b)landmark datasets

Fig. 6. Absolute error of range query under different privacy budget

the largest distribution value is Qopt, which verify the robustness of error analysis and granularity partition model proposed in this paper.

5.3.3 Efficiency

Table 2 and 3 show the running time of different algorithms on storage and landmark dataset. In order to better reflect the differences between different algorithms, the running time in the table does not include the time to read data and query data.

Table 2. Running time of different algorithms on the storage dataset (ms)

Algorithm	ε		
	0.1	0.5	1.0
UG	27.5	34	36
AG	38	36	37
Qopt	400	387	379
Staircase_Ugrid	27	34.5	37.5
Lap_Ugrid	27.5	35	36.5

We can learn from Table 2 and Table 3 that the choice of privacy budget does not affect the running time of kinds of algorithms under the same dataset; The tree structure-based partitioning method Qopt takes longer to run, which is more obvious in small dataset; The Staircase_Ugrid and Laplace_Ugrid are essentially single uniform partition, so the operating efficiency is higher.

Table 3. Running time of different algorithms on the landmark dataset (ms)

Algorithm	ε		
	0.1	0.5	1.0
UG	1310	1228	1201
AG	1630	1480	1315
Qopt	2700	2540	2517
Staircase_Ugrid	1307	1229	1198
Lap_Ugrid	1310	1224	1213

6   Conclusion

In order to improve the publishing accuracy of two-dimensional space division, this paper uses the theoretically optimal noise-adding mechanism that satisfies differential privacy to perturb the counting output. At the same time, a linear least squares fit is used to quantify the relationship between the interacted area and the non-uniform error, and the optimal uniform granularity is obtained by minimizing the two types of errors. Experiments show that this paper proposes an efficient two-dimensional space division method, which makes a good trade-off between data publishing accuracy and time efficiency.

Due to the huge amount of spatial data, the partition methods that are independent of data distribution cannot give consideration to the balance of noise error and non-uniform error. The next work considers the process of density adaptation and designs heuristic rules to distinguish the dense and sparse boundaries of data, so as to improve the accuracy of range queries.

Acknowledgment. This work was supported by the National Natural Science Foundation of China under Grant 61702148 and Grant 61672648.

References

1. Dwork, C.: Differential privacy. In: Bugliesi, M., Preneel, B., Sassone, V., Wegener, I. (eds.) ICALP 2006. LNCS, vol. 4052, pp. 1–12. Springer, Heidelberg (2006). https://doi.org/10.1007/11787006_1
2. Dwork, C.: Differential privacy: a survey of results. In: Agrawal, M., Du, D., Duan, Z., Li, A. (eds.) TAMC 2008. LNCS, vol. 4978, pp. 1–19. Springer, Heidelberg (2008). https://doi.org/10.1007/978-3-540-79228-4_1
3. Qardaji, W., Yang, W., Li, N.: Differentially private grids for geospatial data. In: 2013 IEEE 29th International Conference on Data Engineering (ICDE), pp. 757–768. IEEE, Brisbane (2013)
4. Xiao, Y., Xiong, L., Yuan, C.: Differentially Private Data Release Through Multidimensional Partitioning. In: Jonker, W., Petković, M. (eds.) SDM 2010. LNCS, vol. 6358, pp. 150–168. Springer, Heidelberg (2010). https://doi.org/10.1007/978-3-642-15546-8_11

5. Cormode, G., Procopiuc, C., Srivastava, D., Shen, E., Yu, T.: Differentially private spatial decompositions. In: 2012 IEEE 28th International Conference on Data Engineering, pp. 20–31. IEEE New York (2012)
6. Qardaji, W., Li, N.: Recursive partitioning and summarization: a practical framework for differentially private data publishing. In: Proceedings of the 7th ACM Symposium on Information, Computer and Communications Security, pp. 38–39. ACM, New York (2012)
7. Geng, Q., Kairouz, P., Oh, S., Viswanath, P.: The staircase mechanism in differential privacy. IEEE J. Sel. Top. Sign. Proces. **9**(7), 1176–1184 (2015)
8. Dwork, C., Roth, A.: The algorithmic foundations of differential privacy. Found. Trends® Theor. Comput. Sci. **9**(3–4), 211–407 (2014)
9. Koufogiannis, F., Han, S., Pappas, G.J.: Optimality of the laplace mechanism in differential privacy. arXiv preprint arXiv:1504.00065 (2015)
10. Xiajie, D.: Research on differential privacy adjustable gaussian mechanism for sensitive data gradual release. Master thesis, Northwest A&F University (2017). (in Chinese)
11. Dwork, C.: A firm foundation for private data analysis. Commun. ACM **54**(1), 86–95 (2011)
12. McSherry, F.D.: Privacy integrated queries: an extensible platform for privacy-preserving data analysis. In: Proceedings of the 2009 ACM SIGMOD International Conference on Management of Data, pp. 19–30. ACM, New York (2009)
13. Wang, J., Zhu, R., Liu, S., Cai, Z.: Node location privacy protection based on differentially private grids in industrial wireless sensor networks. Sensors **18**(2), 410 (2018)
14. Dwork, C., McSherry, F., Nissim, K., Smith, A.: Calibrating noise to sensitivity in private data analysis. In: Halevi, S., Rabin, T. (eds.) TCC 2006. LNCS, vol. 3876, pp. 265–284. Springer, Heidelberg (2006). https://doi.org/10.1007/11681878_14
15. Cormode, G., Procopiuc, C., Srivastava, D., et al.: Differentially private spatial decompositions. In: 2012 IEEE 28th International Conference on Data Engineering, pp. 20–31. IEEE, Washington (2012)
16. Rottondi, C., Verticale, G., Capone, A.: Privacy-preserving smart metering with multiple data consumers. Comput. Netw. **57**(7), 1699–1713 (2013)
17. Ahmadi, H., Pham, N., Ganti, R., Abdelzaher, T., Nath, S., Han, J.: Privacy-aware regression modeling of participatory sensing data. In: Proceedings of the 8th ACM Conference on Embedded Networked Sensor Systems, pp. 99–112. ACM (2010)
18. Acar, A., Aksu, H., Uluagac, A.S., et al.: A survey on homomorphic encryption schemes: *Theory and implementation.* Comput. Surv. **51**(4), 1–35 (2018)
19. Li, Q., Cao, G.: Efficient and privacy-preserving data aggregation in mobile sensing. In: 2012 20th IEEE International Conference on Network Protocols, pp. 1–10. IEEE, Austin (2012)
20. Sweeney, L.: k-anonymity: a model for protecting privacy. Int. J. Uncertainty Fuzziness Knowl. Based Syst. **10**(05), 557–570 (2002)
21. Machanavajjhala, A., Kifer, D., Gehrke, J., et al.: L-diversity: privacy beyond k-anonymity. ACM Trans. Knowl. Discov. From Data **1**(1), 3-es (2006)
22. Wong, R.C.W., Fu, A.W.C., Wang, K., et al.: Can the utility of anonymized data be used for privacy breaches. ACM Trans. Knowl. Discovery From Data (TKDD) **5**(3), 1–24 (2011)
23. Wang, J., Wang, L., Wang, Y., et al.: Task allocation in mobile crowd sensing: State-of-the-art and future opportunities. IEEE Internet Things J. **5**(5), 3747–3757 (2018)

A Visualization Analysis Approach for Logistics Customer Maintenance

Yang Liu$^{(\boxtimes)}$ and Ting Jiang

JD Logistics, Beijing, China
{liuyang130,jiangting}@jd.com

Abstract. Customer maintenance plays a critical role in operating the logistics corporations. Motivated by the recent massive employment of data science in this field, analysts tend to solve customer maintenance problems using predictive modeling. Furthermore, data visualization is usually utilized as an interactive tool to involve domain knowledge in data-driven analysis to select highly relevant features for the sake of improving accuracy and reducing computational complexity. While approaches have been developed to observe the importance of features, it is of great interest to know how they impact the experience of customers. The existing methods such as scatterplot and paralleled coordinate plot for visualizing the correlation between attributes do not have a deep view of the data and the interpretation capability is limited. To address this issue, this paper investigates the underlying correlation between continuous features and binary class labels to facilitate classification modeling. A data visualization analysis framework is developed using weight of evidence (WOE), where a semi-supervised approach is proposed to discretize the continuous features for WOE computation targeting on the appropriate discovery and visualization of hidden data patterns. As shown in the experimental results, the developed visualization analysis framework demonstrates a superior interpretation capability compared to the existing methods.

Keywords: Logistics service · Customer maintenance · Data visualization · Feature selection · Continuous variable discretization

1 Introduction

Machine learning technology has been widely employed in the logistics and transportation industry to process huge volume of data for the improvement of customer experience in recent years. An accurate modeling of customer experience is usually nontrivial since it can be impacted by a variety of factors such as transportation delay, economical cost, etc. In order to tackle the challenges induced by complex data structure and high data dimension, a press of research has been conducted, among which feature selection method can effectively remove weak informative features and noise to improve accuracy and reduce computational

© Springer Nature Singapore Pte Ltd. 2020
J. Wang et al. (Eds.): GPC 2020 Workshops, CCIS 1311, pp. 18–30, 2020.
https://doi.org/10.1007/978-981-33-4532-4_2

complexity [8, 16]. The term "feature" refers to the mathematical representation of a factor considered for modeling. The existing research in this direction can be divided into two classes. The first class measures the importance of features based on statistical criteria and subsequently select subsets of important features using a search method [8, 15]. The second class employs data visualization to involve human experience and domain knowledge and draw insights from the visualized form of data [12].

Data visualization is a long existing research topic that bridges the machine learning algorithms and analysts. Compared to fully data-driven methods, it provides more intuitive feedback and allows analysts to discover the informative data patterns based on observation. On the other hand, the predictive models are important to be interpretable as well as accurate in practice [13]. Therefore, various research works have been conducted to explore the meaningful features assisted by data visualization. In [16], high dimensional data is projected to a radial axis that presents the impact of features to facilitate backward selection. In [5], data visualization is studied collaborated with support vector machine to explore the best projection of variables that can separate different class labels. In [13], a tree-structured Bayesian network is proposed to balance prediction power and interpretability by simultaneous classification, feature selection and visualization. In [19], two data visualization methods are proposed to find interesting feature coordinate projections based on joint mutual information and independent component analysis, respectively. In [3], the quality metric for visualization is studied to identify useful feature dimensions.

While efforts have been spent on discovering the importance of features, it is of great interest to know the physical impact of features to the model. For instance, customer maintenance is a crucial task for logistics corporations, where people desire to correctly understand customers' need from the data. In fact, several tools have been developed to observe the relationships between variables, among which scatterplot, pixel-oriented visualization and paralleled coordinate plot are most common [1, 4, 9–11]. However, these visualization techniques present the data form without deep investigations and rely too much on human efforts to observe the patterns. For this reason, the capabilities of these methods are usually limited when recognizing complex relationships. To tackle the aforementioned difficulties, we aim to aid data visualization using machine learning and information theoretic techniques. We target on extracting the underlying relationships between variables and reveal the hidden pattern of data for visualization.

This paper focuses on developing a framework to discover and visualize the underlying relationships between features and binary class labels. Weight of evidence (WOE) is utilized as the tool to help represent the discovered data pattern. WOE is first defined in [18] based on the probability of occurrence and has been adopted in various domains such as risk analysis [17]. While analyzing a feature using WOE, the data samples are usually arranged into discrete bins and the logarithm of positive/negative proportion ratios are computed in each bin as WOE [2, 14]. Subsequently, analysts can explore the impact of the feature by observing the trend of WOE values. While the bins are naturally existed for discrete valued features, appropriate discretization is a crucial task for continuous-valued features such that the impact of features can be correctly revealed by the computed WOE. The existing continuous feature discretization methods separate the feature value into discrete spaces relying on either the distribution of feature value or the guidance of class labels and thereby can be classified into unsupervised and supervised approaches [6]. However, the relationship between a feature and class label cannot be easily extracted with these methods in practice due to the limitations induced by interference from other data dimensions, nonideality and noise, thereby inducing incorrect understanding of the data. For instance, it is intuitive that customer experience should degrade when quality-of-service (QoS) decreases. Yet, the trend of WOE values may not be able to present it perfectly since the price usually decreases as well when the QoS is lower, which can compensate the reduction of customer experience induced by QoS degradation. Thus, we desire to discretize the feature value appropriately such that the interference of price can be eliminated and the correlation between QoS and customer experience can be clearly observed.

In contrast to the existing methods, a semi-supervised approach is proposed in this paper to facilitate WOE visualization by optimizing continuous feature discretization. It contains the supervised discritezation step that generates an initial discretization considering class label information and unsupervised merging step that improves the discretization result based on the distribution of WOE values. An information theoretic monotonicity analysis technique is also developed to reduce the solution space such that different types of correlations can be handled by a generic method. Thus, the contributions of this work are summarized as follows.

- A data visualization analysis framework is developed using WOE to discover the underlying relationships between continuous-valued features and binary class labels.
- A semi-supervised approach is proposed for continuous feature discretization to facilitate the computation of WOE for appropriate presentation of data patterns.
- Information theoretic method is used for monotonicity analysis to enhance the capability of the proposed method for visualizing different types of relationships.
- Comparative study is conducted on JD Logistics customer service data against two existing methods, where the developed visualization framework demonstrates a superior capability on interpreting hidden data patterns.

The reminder of this paper is organized as follows. The definition and application context of WOE are briefly introduced in Sect. 2. The developed data visualization analysis framework is presented in details in Sect. 3. Comparative studies are conducted and the experimental results are discussed in Sect. 4. Finally, we conclude in Sect. 5.

2   Preliminaries

Suppose that we are given a set of data samples S with a continuous-valued feature, represented by $x = \{x_1, x_2, \ldots, x_n\}$ and a binary class label represented by $y = \{y_1, y_2, \ldots, y_n\}$, $y_i \in \{0,1\}, \forall i \in [1,n]$. Let the data samples be divided into ordinal bins indexed by B_i that $i \in [1,m]$ according to the value of x. The weight of evidence (WOE) of bin B_i is computed by

$$WOE_{B_i} = \log \frac{n_{i,1}/n_1}{n_{i,0}/n_0}, \tag{1}$$

where $n_{i,1}$ and $n_{i,0}$ are the numbers of positive and negative samples in bin B_i, n_1 and n_0 are the total numbers of positive and negative samples [14].

Subsequently, the analysts can identify the relationship between x and y by observing the trend of WOE values. For example, if the WOE value increases when moving to a bin with larger feature values, x and y are positively correlated.

In practice, the relationship between feature and class label is usually not easy to observe due to interference from other dimensions, nonideality and noise. Refer to the example in Paragraph 4 of Sect. 1. Since the WOE value is strongly relevant to the bin arrangement, an appropriate discretization approach can help WOE to correctly present the hidden data patterns. However, although various continuous value discretization methods have been studied, none of them has explored the underlying correlations in depth.

3   Feature Discretization

This section investigates the discretizaiton of continuous-valued features to facilitate the visualization of feature&label correlation using WOE. The proposed method contains two steps. In the first step, the initial discretization is computed by extracting the supervised information from class labels. Subsequently, the correlation type between the feature and label is identified and a novel unsupervised method is used to re-arrange the discretization result to match the recognized pattern of WOE.

3.1   Supervised Discretization

In this part, a supervised approach presented in [7] is deployed to generate an initial discretization of the continuous features. That method pursues partitions of feature values that can optimize information gain. Furthermore, coding theory is used to define the stopping criterion to avoid artificial tuning of hyperparameters. The main steps are included as follows [6,7].

– Given the continuous feature x and binary class label y, sort the data samples according to the feature values in ascending order.

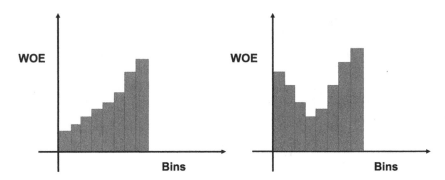

Fig. 1. Monotonic correlation and U-shaped correlation.

– Identify the set of candidate cut points as the boundaries of classes since it contains the cut point that carries the largest amount of information [7]. A cut point refers to a partition that separates a continuous range into two discrete bins.
– For a candidate cut point T, define the information gain as

$$E(S, T, \boldsymbol{x}) = \frac{|S_1|}{|S|} Ent(S_1) + \frac{|S_2|}{|S|} Ent(S_2), \qquad (2)$$

where S_1 and S_2 are the subsets of data samples resulting from applying cut point T to S. $Ent(S_1)$ and $Ent(S_2)$ are the entropy values of S_1 and S_2 defined in [7].
– Select the candidate point $T_{min} = \arg\min_T \{E(S, T, \boldsymbol{x})\}$ and apply it to partition the data samples. Apply this recursively to all the generated subsets until stopping criterion is reached.
– For a subset S', the optimal cut point T' is rejected iff

$$Ent(S') - E(S', T', \boldsymbol{x}') < \frac{\log |S'| - 1}{|S'|} + \frac{\Delta(\boldsymbol{x}', T', S')}{|S'|}, \qquad (3)$$

where
$$\begin{aligned} \Delta(\boldsymbol{x}', T', S') = \log(3^k - 2) \\ - [k \cdot Ent(S') - k_1 \cdot Ent(S_1') - k_2 \cdot Ent(S_2')]. \end{aligned} \qquad (4)$$

S_1' and S_2' are the subsets of S' resulting from applying T'. k, k_1 and k_2 are the number of distinct class labels contained in S', S_1' and S_2', respectively. Equation (4) means that the gain achieved by applying T' to S' is lower than the cost to describe the partition. In this situation, S' will not be partitioned.

3.2   Unsupervised Merging

After the initial discretization in Subsect. 3.1, the WOE values can already be computed according to Eq. (1) for analyzing the feature. However, due to the interference induced by other dimensions, nonideality and noise, the pattern of WOE values cannot perfectly represent the correlation between feature and class label. Thus, an unsupervised merging method is proposed to recognize the correlation from the ambiguous pattern of initial discretization result. Subsequently, the recognized correlation is matched by merging the bins with similar properties.

Monotonicity Analysis. Given the initial discretization result, we aim to recognize the specific correlation between feature and class label. In practice, we mainly consider two types of correlations, i.e., monotonic correlation and U-shaped correlation since they are the most common correlations in reality. For monotonic correlation, the WOE value increases/decreases monotonically as the feature value increases. Thus, the WOE value is monotonic to the index of bins. For U-shaped correlation, the WOE value first increases and then decreases or first decreases and then increases as the feature value increases. Thus, while the feature value increases, the pattern of WOE values is similar to the letter "U". Refer to Fig. 1. In addition, these correlations can be further classified into positive monotonic correlation, negative monotonic correlation, downward U-shaped correlation and upward U-shaped correlation.

Since there exists multiple types of correlations, we need to recognize the specific correlation type among multiple options from still ambiguous WOE pattern from initial discretization. Furthermore, the proposed visualization method should be able to handle different potential correlations coherently to avoid increasing the solution complexity. In order to tackle these challenges, a monotonicity analysis method is proposed based on information theory. It explores the similarities between different correlation types and discover a generic solution.

It is obvious to observe from Fig. 1 that for both monotonic correlation and U-shaped correlation, the WOE value pattern can be divided into two monotonic spaces. Based on this observation, we aim to find the cut point to partition the bins into two near-monotonic spaces and tune each space separately to match the approximated trend. Hence, an important task is to find that cut point. In order to fulfill this task, we take the trend sequence of the WOE values as $[tr_1, tr_2, \ldots, tr_{m-1}]$ such that for bins B_i and B_{i+1}, the trend tr_i is computed by

$$tr_i = \mathbf{sign}(WOE_{B_{i+1}} - WOE_{B_i}), \tag{5}$$

where WOE_{B_i} is the WOE value of bin B_i. Thus, each entry in the trend sequence yields $tr_i \in \{-1, 1\}$, where 1 represents an increasing local monotonicity between B_i and B_{i+1} and -1 represents a decreasing local monotonicity. Based on this definition, the optimal cut point should be the location that partitions the WOE sequence into two sub-sequences and make the trend sequences of each one as consistent as possible. Refer to Fig. 2. This target can be reached by minimizing the information gain for partitioning trend sequence $[tr_1, tr_2, \ldots, tr_{m-1}]$, where information gain is defined in Eq. (2). A simple linear search can be applied to all the boundaries between the bins to find the optimal cut point.

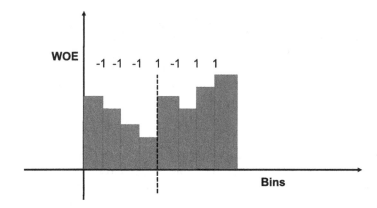

Fig. 2. Partition the bins into two sub-spaces based on information gain where the WOE values of both sub-sequences are near-monotonic.

After partitioning, we directly take the majority of the local monotonicity as the global monotonicity of each sub-space such that the global monotonicity m_g is computed by

$$m_g = \mathbf{mode}(tr_i), \forall i \in B^s \tag{6}$$

where B^s is a sub-space of bins. For instance, if most of the entries in the trend sequence are 1, we assume the global monotonicity of that sub-space is increasing.

Bin Re-Arranging. After recognizing the monotonicity, the discretization in each sub-space is re-arranged to match it. The basic logic of the proposed method is to find the locations whose local monotonicity is inconsistent with the global monotonicity and modify it through re-arranging the bins. There are two targets for re-arranging: improving monotonicity and merging the bins with similar properties. In order to clearly describe our strategy, we consider a specific example as follows.

Suppose that the value of the feature to be visualized is discretized into several bins by supervised discretization method. The WOE values of the bins are shown in Fig. 3, where the global monotonicity is increasing while the local monotonicity between bins B_{i-1} and B_i is decreasing.

It is intuitive that B_i is the bin we need to handle since it violates the global monotonicity. We aim to resolve this issue by merging B_i to an adjacent bin, i.e., B_{i-1} or B_{i+1}. In order to determine the specific bin that B_i merges to, our strategy is to compute the WOE values of $B_i \bigcup B_{i-1}$ and $B_i \bigcup B_{i+1}$ as $WOE_{B_i \bigcup B_{i-1}}$ and $WOE_{B_i \bigcup B_{i+1}}$, respectively. Subsequently, we compare $|WOE_{B_i \bigcup B_{i-1}} - WOE_{B_i}|$ and $|WOE_{B_i \bigcup B_{i+1}} - WOE_{B_i}|$, select

---

Algorithm 1. WOE Based Bin Re-Arranging.

1: Given a set of discrete bins $\{B_1, B_2, \ldots, B_m\}$, compute the WOE values as $WOE_{B_i}, \forall B_i \in \{B_1, B_2, \ldots, B_m\}$ and the local monotinicities as $\{tr_i\}, \forall i \in [1, m-1]$.

2: Compute global monotonicity as $m_g = \mathbf{mode}(tr_i)$.

3: **while** $\exists i : \{tr_i\} \neq m_g$ **do**

4:      Compute the set of bins to be handled as $\{B_j\}, \forall \{tr_{j-1}\} \neq m_g$ and $\{tr_j\} = m_g$

5:      Compute $WOE_{B_j}^{diff}, \forall B_j \in \{B_j\}$ according to Equation (8)

6:      Find the bin to be merged in this iteration according to Equation (9) as B_θ

7:      Find the bin to be merged to B_θ according to Equation (7) as B_θ^*

8:      Merge B_θ and B_θ^* into one bin

9:      Update bin indices

10:     Update WOE values $WOE_{B_i}, \forall i$

11:     Update local monotonicities $tr_i, \forall i$

12: **end while**

$$B_i^* = \arg \min_{B \in \{B_{i-1}, B_{i+1}\}} \{|WOE_{B_i \cup B_{i-1}} - WOE_{B_i}|,$$
$$|WOE_{B_i \cup B_{i+1}} - WOE_{B_i}|\}, \tag{7}$$

and merge it to B_i since $B_i^* \bigcup B_i$ has a similar distribution to B_i. The difference between WOE_{B_i} and $WOE_{B_i^* \cup B_i}$ is denoted by

$$WOE_i^{diff} = |WOE_{B_i \cup B_i^*} - WOE_{B_i}|. \tag{8}$$

Note that there can be multiple local inconsistencies. Thus, an iterative approach is proposed such that in each iteration the bin to be merged is selected by

$$B^* = \arg \min_{B_i} \{WOE_i^{diff}\}. \tag{9}$$

It is then merged to a bin selected according to Eq. (7). The selecting and merging are repeated until all the local monotonicities are consistent with the global monotonicity.

There may exist a bin B_i where the monotonicity between both $\{B_{i-1}, B_i\}$ and $\{B_i, B_{i+1}\}$ do not match the global monotonicity such that $tr_{i-1} \neq m_g$ and $tr_i \neq m_g$. In this scenario, we skip this type of bins and choose the bins where $tr_{i-1} \neq m_g$ and $tr_i = m_g$ since modifying that type of bins is the fastest way to improve the monotonicity. In order to show this, we suppose that in bins B_{i-1} and B_i, the number of positive samples are denoted by $n_{i-1,1}$ and $n_{i,1}$, respectively. Similarly, the number of negative samples are denoted by $n_{i-1,0}$ and $n_{i,0}$, respectively. Assume that the total number of positive and negative samples in the data set are n_1 and n_0. Thus, the WOE values of bins B_{i-1} and B_i are computed by

$$WOE_{B_{i-1}} = \log \left(\frac{n_{i-1,1}/n_1}{n_{i-1,0}/n_0} \right) \tag{10}$$

and

$$WOE_{B_i} = \log\left(\frac{n_{i,1}/n_1}{n_{i,0}/n_0}\right). \tag{11}$$

The WOE value of $B_{i-1}\bigcup B_i$ is computed by

$$WOE_{B_{i-1}\bigcup B_i} = \log\left[\frac{(n_{i-1,1}+n_{i,1})/n_1}{(n_{i-1,0}+n_{i,0})/n_0}\right]. \tag{12}$$

Considering the properties of logarithm operation, we can directly compare $WOE_{B_{i-1}}$ and $WOE_{B_{i-1}\bigcup B_i}$ by comparing $\frac{n_{i-1,1}}{n_{i-1,0}}$ and $\frac{n_{i-1,1}+n_{i,1}}{n_{i-1,0}+n_{i,0}}$. Similarly, we can compare WOE_{B_i} and $WOE_{B_{i-1}\bigcup B_i}$ by comparing $\frac{n_{i,1}}{n_{i,0}}$ and $\frac{n_{i-1,1}+n_{i,1}}{n_{i-1,0}+n_{i,0}}$. It is easy to derive that

$$\frac{n_{i-1,1}+n_{i,1}}{n_{i-1,0}+n_{i,0}} - \frac{n_{i-1,1}}{n_{i-1,0}} = \frac{n_{i,1}n_{i-1,0}-n_{i-1,1}n_{i,0}}{(n_{i-1,0}+n_{i,0})n_{i-1,0}} \tag{13}$$

and

$$\frac{n_{i-1,1}+n_{i,1}}{n_{i-1,0}+n_{i,0}} - \frac{n_{i,1}}{n_{i,0}} = \frac{n_{i-1,1}n_{i,0}-n_{i,1}n_{i-1,0}}{(n_{i-1,0}+n_{i,0})n_{i,0}}. \tag{14}$$

Since

$$(n_{i,1}n_{i-1,0}-n_{i-1,1}n_{i,0}) \times (n_{i-1,1}n_{i,0}-n_{i,1}n_{i-1,0}) \leq 0, \tag{15}$$

the value of $WOE_{B_{i-1}\bigcup B_i}$ must be between $WOE_{B_{i-1}}$ and WOE_{B_i}. Refer to Fig. 3. Suppose that B_i is the bin that violates the global monotonicity, merging bins B_{i-1} and B_i can either improve the monotonicity condition or reduce the differences between adjacent bins to ease the monotonicity improvement in next iteration.

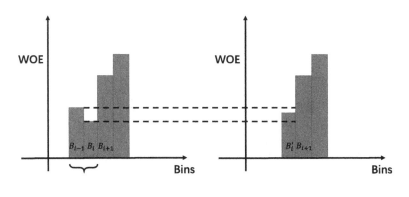

Fig. 3. The WOE values of adjacent bins and the WOE value after merging.

Thus, the main steps of the proposed algorithm are summarized in Algorithm 1. After executing Algorithm 1, the monotonicity of the re-arranged bins is analyzed again using the method in Part 3.2 and Algorithm 1 is executed again if there still exists local inconsistencies. This is repeated until no further change can be applied to the discretization result. Considering both the supervised discretization step and unsupervised merging step, the main steps of our semi-supervised continuous feature discretization technique are summarized in Algorithm 2.

Algorithm 2. Semi-Supervised Continuous Feature Discretization.

1: Given a set of data samples, obtain the continuous feature to be analyze x and binary label y.
2: Execute the continuous feature discretization method in [7] to generate initial discretization.
3: **repeat**
4:    Use the method in Part 3.2 to separate the initial discrete bins into two parts and analyze the monotonicity in each part.
5:    Execute Algorithm 1 to re-arrange the bins in each part.
6: **until** No further change can be applied to the discretization result.

After executing Algorithm 2, the final discretization result is achieved. Subsequently, the WOE value in each bin can be computed and visualized. Analysts can determine the relationship between the continuous feature and binary class label though observing the pattern of WOE values.

4 Case Study

In this section, visualization analysis is conducted on the customer service data of JD Logistics. This task aims to suggest a set of customers that need maintenance and the developed visualization analysis framework can help explore the potential dimensions relevant to customer experience. In order to demonstrate the efficacy of our proposed technique, two existing methods are used for comparative study, which are equal interval discretization [6] and information gain based discretization [7]. The dataset contains 21182 positive samples and 61006 negative samples, where a positive sample represent a customer that needs maintenance. Two features denoted by "feature 1" and "feature 2" are selected for visualization study. For confidential issue, the physical meanings of these features are hidden. The visualization results of feature 1 and feature 2 are shown in Fig. 4 and Fig. 5, respectively. As shown in the experimental results, the proposed technique clearly recognizes and visualizes the monotonic correlation of feature 1 such that the WOE value increases when the feature value increases. Similarly, U-shaped correlation is observed for feature 2. Compared to the existing methods in citech2disc and citech2multi, the proposed method demonstrates a superior capability on discovering the underlying relationship between feature and label.

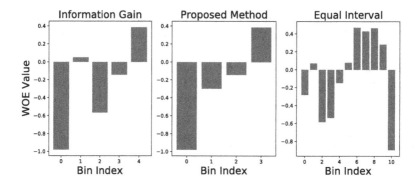

Fig. 4. Visualization results for feature 1, monotonic correlation is recognized.

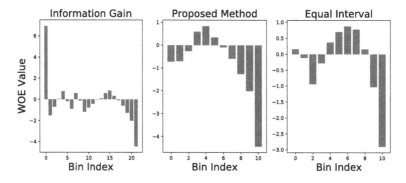

Fig. 5. Visualization results for feature 2, U-shaped correlation is recognized.

Subsequently, feature 1 and feature 2 can be selected for modeling to predict the customers that need maintenance since they have strong correlations with the customer experience. After these customers are recognized, the WOE of the features for modeling can be further utilized to suggest the specific aspects for maintenance. According to the definition of WOE, a positive WOE value means a higher positive/negative ratio than that of the whole dataset. Therefore, if a customer is within the range with positive WOE value on a feature, this feature illustrates a factor that degrades the experience of that customer. Hence, logistics corporations can improve the quality of services corresponding to the suggested features of that customer, thereby improving the customer experience.

5   Conclusion and Future Work

In this paper, a data visualization analysis framework is developed based on weight of evidence (WOE) to facilitate the analysis of continuous-valued features in classification tasks. A semi-supervised approach is proposed to appropriately discretize a continuous feature such that the underlying relationship between the feature and class label can be correctly presented by the pattern of WOE values.

The proposed method is applied to the improvement of customer experience for logistics service. Compared to the existing methods for continuous feature discretization, the proposed method is more effective on discovering the underlying relationships, thereby providing an insightful interpretation of the data. While this paper is dedicated in the visualization analysis of a single feature, analysts also would like to investigate the joint impact of multiple features to the class label. This will be an important future research task of us.

References

1. Anderson, R.K.: Visual Data Mining: The VisMiner Approach. John Wiley & Sons, Hoboken (2012)
2. Ba, Q., Chen, Y., Deng, S., Wu, Q., Yang, J., Zhang, J.: An improved information value model based on gray clustering for landslide susceptibility mapping. ISPRS Int. J. Geo-Inf. **6**(1), 18 (2017)
3. Bertini, E., Tatu, A., Keim, D.: Quality metrics in high-dimensional data visualization: an overview and systematization. IEEE Trans. Vis. Comput. Graph. **17**(12), 2203–2212 (2011)
4. Cleveland, W.S.: Visualizing Data. Hobart Press, Thousand Oaks (1993)
5. Cook, D., Caragea, D., Honavar, V.: Visualization for classification problems, with examples using support vector machines. In: Proceedings of the COMPSTAT (2004)
6. Dougherty, J., Kohavi, R., Sahami, M.: Supervised and unsupervised discretization of continuous features. In: Machine Learning Proceedings 1995, pp. 194–202. Elsevier (1995)
7. Fayyad, U., Irani, K.: Multi-interval discretization of continuous-valued attributes for classification learning. In: Proceedings of International Joint Conference on Artificial Intelligence (1993)
8. Gadat, S., Younes, L.: A stochastic algorithm for feature selection in pattern recognition. J. Mach. Learn. Res. **8**, 509–547 (2007)
9. Inselberg, A., Dimsdale, B.: Parallel coordinates: a tool for visualizing multidimensional geometry. In: Proceedings of IEEE Conference on Visualization: Visualization 1990, pp. 361–378 (Oct 1990)
10. Itoh, T., Kumar, A., Klein, K., Kim, J.: High-dimensional data visualization by interactive construction of low-dimensional parallel coordinate plots. J. Vis. Lang. Comput. **43**, 1–13 (2017)
11. Keim, D.A.: Designing pixel-oriented visualization techniques: theory and applications. IEEE Trans. Vis. Comput. Graph. **6**(1), 59–78 (2000)
12. Keim, D.A.: Information visualization and visual data mining. IEEE Trans. Vis. Comput. Graph. **8**(1), 1–8 (2002)
13. Krakovna, V., Du, J., Liu, J.S.: Interpretable selection and visualization of features and interactions using bayesian forests. arXiv preprint arXiv:1506.02371 (2015)
14. Lin, A.Z.: Using information value, information gain and gain ratio for detecting two-way interaction effect (2018)
15. Liu, Y., Li, X.: Predictive modeling for advanced virtual metrology: a tree-based approach. In: Proceedings of International Conference on Emerging Technologies and Factory Automation, vol. 1, pp. 845–852 (2018)

16. Sánchez, A., Soguero-Ruiz, C., Mora-Jiménez, I., Rivas-Flores, F.J., Lehmann, D., Rubio-Sánchez, M.: Scaled radial axes for interactive visual feature selection: a case study for analyzing chronic conditions. Expert Syst. Appl. **100**, 182–196 (2018)
17. Weed, D.L.: Weight of evidence: a review of concept and methods. Risk Anal. Int. J. **25**(6), 1545–1557 (2005)
18. Wod, I.: Weight of evidence: a brief survey. Bayesian Stat. **2**(2), 249–270 (1985)
19. Yang, H.H., Moody, J.: Data visualization and feature selection: new algorithms for nongaussian data. In: Proceedings of Advances in Neural Information Processing Systems, pp. 687–693 (2000)

Short-Term Traffic Speed Prediction
via Machine Learning

Luis Romo[1], Jingru Zhang[2(✉)], Kevin Eastin[1], and Chao Xue[3]

[1] University of Texas-Rio Grande Valley, Edinburg, TX, USA
[2] Cleveland State University, Cleveland, OH, USA
j.zhang40@csuohio.edu
[3] Chang'an University, Xi'an, China

Abstract. Short-term traffic speed prediction is a key component of Intelligent Transportation Systems (ITS), which has an impact on travelers' routing decisions and behaviors to the traffic congestion. In the past years, traffic speed prediction has been studied a lot and different machine learning methods are employed, including deep learning approaches, which recently attracts much attention from both academic and industry fields. In this work, we investigate three different machine learning methods for predicting the short-term traffic speed, i.e., Convolutional Neural Network, Long Short-term Memory Neural Network and Extreme Gradient Boost. The training and testing data are collected by ourselves from the California Department of Transportation. Through comparisons with the baseline average method, it is obvious that machine learning approaches can achieve more accurate and stable prediction performance.

1 Introduction

Tracking traffic congestion is an important challenge faced by the city management all over the world. Better management of traffic congestion can lead to a more effective use of the city's fuel resources as well as increase the convenience of travel by reducing commute time. Traffic prediction, especially the short-term prediction (less than 20 min) in traffic flow, speed and density, plays a major role in predicting traffic conditions to control urban traffic [1–3]. In the past decades, plenty of research have been done to forecast the traffic condition to achieve better traffic management. There are a lot of work focusing on utilizing traditional statistic models to describe the traffic flow, such as [4–8]. [9] proposed an online algorithm to predict the medium-term traffic flow by a recursive least-square estimation. For short-term prediction, [10] applied the Bayesian estimator to model traffic flow pattern.

As the widespread deployment of traffic sensors, like inductive loop detector and cameras, the wide availability of traffic data of road network and the power of computation lead that the focus of researches on traffic prediction shifts to a data-intensive era. To reveal that the stochastic nature of traffic data,

© Springer Nature Singapore Pte Ltd. 2020
J. Wang et al. (Eds.): GPC 2020 Workshops, CCIS 1311, pp. 31–42, 2020.
https://doi.org/10.1007/978-981-33-4532-4_3

machine learning techniques have attracted more attention and become more and more popular in traffic prediction as the development of artificial intelligence techniques.

Researches of utilizing machine learning techniques can be traced back to the 1990s, when [11] introduced the Artificial Neural Network (NN) to model the nonlinear property of traffic flow and predicted traffic congestion, which achieved a better performance compared to some traditional methods at that time. From then, more and more machine learning techniques came to view for improving the performance of traffic prediction, such as Modular Neural Network [12], Recurrent Neural Network (RNN) [13, 14] and other variants of Neural Network [15]. To learn the long-term dependencies of time series data, Long Short-term Memory Neural Network (LSTM), a special RNN, was developed and can automatically determine the optimal time lags for prediction. In [16], LSTM was firstly applied to the short-term traffic speed prediction. Specially, [16] constructed a traffic speed dataset with two-minute interval collected by two sensors along a highway, and fed them into LSTM to learn the nonlinear traffic dynamic and predicted the upcoming two-minute interval speed.

Recently, the deep learning theory, specifically, Convolutional Neural Network (CNN) and its variances like Region-based CNN (R-CNN) [17], becomes incredibly effective in solving problems in traffic prediction [18–21]. [22] used a spatio-temporal recurrent convolutional neural network(SRCN) to predict the future state of traffic by modeling traffic condition of an entire road network at a time into a matrix and trained SRCN on those obtained matrices. [23] attempted to predict the average speed of traffic recorded on a sensor five minutes in the future by only using the past 25-minute data. [23] trained a model to predict the future speed recorded any specific sensor based on the previous speed in the last 25 min, broken up into 5-minute intervals of the previous 4 sensors (the current and next four sensors on the road). They then trained a long short-term neural network on that data to create their predictive model. Their purpose was to create a scalable network that can be used to predict the traffic speed of different roads and not be reliant on having access to the historical data of the area.

In this paper, we are interested in short-term traffic speed prediction along certain traffic network points/sensors of the road. In this work, three prevailing machine learning methods are studied: CNN, LSTM and XGBoost. We collected the real traffic speed data from the Caltrans Performance Measurement System (PeMS) [24] in California. We normalize traffic speed data of each traffic network point to 2D matrices and train the three models and test them on our collected data of different sizes. On our collected data, we compare three machine learning methods with the baseline average method for experiments. The experimental results show that the machine learning approaches are more accurate and stable than the baseline average method.

2   Preliminaries

In this section, we will give the definitions of traffic speed prediction problem.

A traffic network is composed of a set of roads and junctions of a given area. Roads are represented as interconnecting lines while junctions, e.g., intersections, entrances and exits of highways, or sensors, are often represented as points. In this project, as Fig. 2 shows, traffic sensors on highways are considered as points because traffic sensors are widely installed on different sections of highway to collect traffic information and average traffic speeds on different sections of highway will be studied in the upstream and downstream direction.

We borrow some terminology from [25]. Denote a network point by s, its adjacent m outflow points on the traffic network by $s-1$, $s-2$, $\cdots$, and $s-m$, which has flow to s, and another m points by $s+1$, $s+2$, $\cdots$, and $s+m$, to which s has flow. Among those points, $s+1$ and $s-1$ are the two closest points to s while $s-m$ and $s+m$ are the farthest.

Let δ denote the time interval during which the average speed at s is computed. Considering a set of time intervals $[t-c\delta, t-(c-1)\delta]$, $[t-(c-2)\delta, t-(c-3)\delta]$, $\cdots$, $[t-\delta, t]$, we are aimed to predict the average speed of s in $[t, t+\delta]$ by using the average speeds of those previous c intervals. For simplicity, we use time t to refer to the time interval from $[t-\delta, t]$. In time dimension, the average speed of a network point S at time $t+1$ is based on its speed data at time $t-c$, $t-c+1$, $t-c+2$, $\cdots$, t.

Considering the spatial interaction of s and $2m$ adjacent network points $s-m$, $\cdots$, $s-1$, $s+1$, $\cdots$, $s+m$ and the impact of traffic flow of them on s, it is necessary to jointly consider traffic information at s in time and space dimensions to predict the average traffic speed of s at time t. Thus, we construct the following time-space speed matrix $x(s,t)$ for a network point s at time t.

$$
\begin{array}{c}
\begin{array}{cccc} t-c & t-c+1 & \cdots & t \end{array} \\
\begin{array}{c} s-m \\ s-m+1 \\ \cdots \\ s \\ \cdots \\ s+m-1 \\ s+m \end{array}
\left[
\begin{array}{cccc}
d_{t-c}^{s-m} & d_{t-c+1}^{s-m} & \cdots & d_t^{s-m} \\
d_{t-c}^{s-m+1} & d_{t-c+1}^{s-m+1} & \cdots & d_t^{s-m+1} \\
\cdots & \cdots & \cdots & \cdots \\
d_{t-c}^{s} & d_{t-c+1}^{s} & \cdots & d_t^{s} \\
\cdots & \cdots & \cdots & \cdots \\
d_{t-c}^{s+m-1} & d_{t-c+1}^{s+m-1} & \cdots & d_t^{s+m-1} \\
d_{t-c}^{s+m} & d_{t-c}^{s+m} & \cdots & d_t^{s+m}
\end{array}
\right]
\end{array}
$$

Where d_β^α is the average speed of a network point α at time β. Given a traffic network $S = \{s_1, s_2, s_3, \cdots, s_n\}$, we denote the time-space speed matrix of S by $X(S,t) = \bigcup_{i=1}^{n} x(s_i, t)$. The goal of the traffic speed prediction problem is to learning a function or network $H(\cdot)$ that maps the historical traffic speed $x(s,t)$ of any network point $s \in S$ to the traffic speed d_{t+1}^s at time $t+1$.

$$
x(s,t) \xrightarrow{H(\cdot)} d_{t+1}^s
$$

3   Methodology

In this section, we develop a machine learning based framework to predict traffic speed of traffic network points. The framework is shown in Fig. 1. We first collect traffic speeds at traffic network points from measurements of sensors, preprocess data to generate time-space speed matrices, partition the generated data set into training data set and test data set, train machine learning models $H(\cdot)$ on the training data set, and examine the performance by predictions on test data set. In this study, we mainly investigate three machine learning methods: Convolutional Neural Network (CNN), Long Short-term Neural Network (LSTM) and Extreme Gradient Boost (XGBoost).

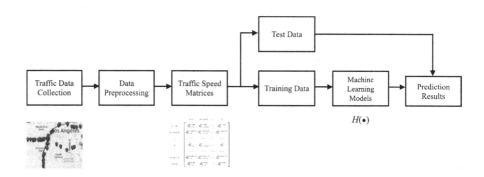

Fig. 1. Illustrating the framework of our experiments.

3.1   Convolutional Neural Network

Convolutional Neural Network (CNN) is a Deep Learning algorithm which can take in a grid format data. Generally, CNN contains three types of layers: convolutional layer, pooling layer and fully connected layer. The convolutional layer, unique to CNN, is composed of layers of neurons. It gets a matrix of the dimensions as input, and performs a convolution computation with a filter on an input matrix of each channel. That is to compute dot products between the entries of the filter and the input at any position, which produces an activation map. In our network structure, one convolutional layer is defined. The output of each neuron is affected by a nonlinear activation function. The output of one convolutional layer is a feature map that consists of n activation maps. The pooling layer is designed for data down sampling which performs a max or average computation over the feature maps by sliding a filter on the feature map to extract the most important spatio-temporal features. Since the input size for the short-term traffic speed prediction is quite small (e.g., 9×5), we ignore the pooling layers in our CNN structure. The fully connected layer, similar to that in an artificial neural network, takes a vector in dimensions as the input, reduces the dimensions, and outputs the result of a vector. After the convolutional layer, we adapts two fully connected layers fc_1 and fc_2. Specifically, we flatten the feature map into one-dimension feature vector and then input it to fc_1 to reduce the dimension to one 4D feature vector, then input it to fc_2 to reduce the dimension to one 1D value as the final prediction.

All the network weights are learned by minimizing the loss function with the backward propagation algorithm, which reflects the error between the model estimation and the actual ground-truth data. In this study, we use the mean square error (MSE) as the loss to train the CNN.

3.2   Long Short-Term Neural Network

As described above, traffic speed prediction is a time-series problem, which are dependent on the previous traffic condition of its neighboring points and itself. We thus employ the Long Short-term Memory neural network (LSTM) to learn the model. LSTM, as a type of recurrent neural network(RNN), solves the long-term dependence problem of RNN for time series data. One LSTM unit is composed of the following components: a cell, a input gate, a forget gate and a output gate. LSTM is featured with this cell, which is the memory part and allows information quickly travel through one step to another. The other three gates take the flattened vector of $x(s,t)$ and the output of last step, i.e., the estimated speed at time $t-1$, both as the input, update the cell state and produce the result.

In our LSTM network, we utilize two LSTM blocks and add one dropout layer after each LSTM block. In our LSTM block, each neural net of every gate contains 20 neurons. To prevent from overfitting, a dropout layer is employed to each LSTM block, in the training process, which randomly drops out the output of some neurons of the prior layer. Note that the dropout layer has no parameter to learn.

3.3   XGBoost

XGBoost [26] is a gradient-boosted decision tree algorithm. A XGBoost structure consists of a series of (splitting) nodes, in terms of the value of an input feature. The root node takes the input, i.e., the flattened $x(s,t)$ in our project, and the last node is a leaf and gives us the estimation. It makes predictions on an output variable by following a series of rules arranged in those nodes. Moreover, XGBoost utilized a gradient boosting algorithm to learn those rules by minimizing the MSE loss function.

Specifically, using the idea of decision tree ensembles, the tree ensemble model consists of a set of classification and regression trees (CART) in XGBoost [26]. By the supervised learning, the training loss and regularization term are jointly minimized to learn the tree structure. When the optimal tree structure is learned during training, it can be further utilized to predict the new testing data for short-term traffic speed prediction.

4 Empirical Study

4.1 Data Collection

The data was collected by ourselves through the California Department of Transportation, known as Caltrans which provides traffic flow information to the public through the California Performance Measurement System (PeMS). PeMS consists of over 40,000 individual detectors covering freeways across metropolitan areas of the State of California and provides over ten years of archived historical data[24].

For this set of experiments, data for average speed and traffic flow (the amount of vehicles that have moved through a specific point on the road) were collected. For the training set, average Speed records of every 5 min interval between January 1, 2017 and July 1, 2017 from 30 traffic network points are collected from PeMS. There were 2016 5-min intervals per week and 1,572,480 records in total. The location of the sensors for the training set and testing set can be seen on the map in Fig. 2. For the testing set, 4 random weeks between January 1, 2018 and July 1, 2018 for the same 30 sensors are gathered. The size of the testing set is 8,064 records.

Missing Data: Due to sensor malfunction, less than 1% of traffic data is missing for a small time step. In our experiments, we fill the miss data by the average of the previous and next records.

4.2 Data Preprocessing

As shown in the preliminary part, the data are represented as time-space matrices, referred as snapshots. These snapshots are two dimensional arrays filled with traffic speed data. The rows indicates which network point the time series data belongs to while the columns indicate at which time step the data is gathered. As one example shown in Fig. 3, to predict the average traffic speed of every network point s at time $t + 5$, we consider the traffic impact of its 4 inflow and outflow consecutive network points and itself in previous 5 time steps, i.e., the average speed of consecutive network points $s - 4$, $s - 3$, $s - 2$, $s - 1$, s, $s + 1$, $s + 2$, $s + 3$, and $s + 4$ respectively at time $t - 20$, $t - 15$, $t - 10$, $t - 5$ and t. So the size of this snapshot is 9×5. In the experiments, different size of snapshots will be explored to pursue a better performance.

4.3 Parameters Setting

In this section, we will introduce the detailed parameter settings for different machine learning models, evaluation metrics, and the baseline method.

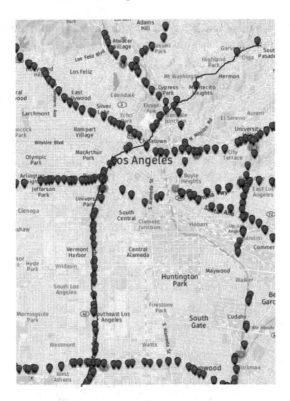

Fig. 2. Map of I-110 Los Angeles Downtown. It is shown as the blue line in this figure, containing the speed detection sensors.

	t-20	t-15	t-10	t-5	t
s-4	66.9	66.3	64.6	65.9	65.6
s-3	69.1	68.6	69.2	66.7	68.5
s-2	68.5	68	66.1	67.6	67.1
s-1	70.1	69.3	68.4	62.7	62.8
s	72.2	65.1	61.1	68.4	66.2
s+1	64.8	63.8	64.7	70.1	69.6
s+2	62.6	61.3	62	70.5	70.5
s+3	70.4	69.9	70.4	70.5	70.5
s+4	61.4	61.7	61.8	62.2	61.4

Fig. 3. Illustrating one input snapshot of size 9×5 for predicting traffic speed of the network point s at time $t + 5$.

CNN: Our CNN network is a five-layer architectures which contains input, convolution, two fully connected, output layers in order. For the convolution layer, the filter size is 3×3 and the total number of filter is 64. The striding is 1 and we use the same for padding. The output of convolution layer is flattened and fed to the fully connected layer. After this layer, the output is 4×1 vector and then the last fully connected layer give the estimated value with this input vector.

Table 1. Errors of traffic speed prediction under four different time steps. Best results are shown in bold.

9x1	MSE	L1	RMSE
XGBoost	10.02	1.92	3.16
CNN	**8.61**	**1.62**	**2.93**
LSTM	24.87	3.66	4.98
Baseline: Average	76.45	6.10	8.45

9x2	MSE	L1	RMSE
XGBoost	**7.99**	**1.59**	**2.82**
CNN	8.58	1.63	2.92
LSTM	17.68	3.20	4.20
Baseline: Average	77.54	6.15	8.80

9x3	MSE	L1	RMSE
XGBoost	**8.06**	**1.61**	**2.83**
CNN	8.47	1.64	2.91
LSTM	17.98	3.01	4.24
Baseline: Average	78.89	6.21	8.88

9x4	MSE	L1	RMSE
XGBoost	**7.95**	**1.59**	**2.82**
CNN	8.63	1.69	2.93
LSTM	16.76	3.06	4.09
Baseline: Average	80.39	6.28	8.96

LSTM: In our LSTM architecture, the six layers in order are input, LSTM, dropout, LSTM, dropout, output layers. In this structure, each snapshot is flattened into one vector, e.g., 9×5 to 45×1, and connect it to the input layer of 45 neurons. For LSTM block, we set the hidden units as 20 (20 neurons of each gate) and use the linear activation function for the output layer.

XGBoost: For XGBoost model, we limits the max tree depth by 5, set a learning rate as 0.5, and the alpha value as 10. Another parameter is the subsample ratio of columns for constructing each tree, and 0.9 is used.

Table 2. Errors of traffic speed prediction under different neighboring point/sensor numbers. Best results are shown in bold.

1x5	MSE	L1	RMSE
XGBoost	9.33	1.78	3.05
CNN	**8.77**	**1.62**	**2.96**
LSTM	30.10	4.84	5.48
Baseline: Average	82.00	5.88	6.35

3x5	MSE	L1	RMSE
XGBoost	**8.57**	1.69	**2.92**
CNN	8.63	**1.65**	2.93
LSTM	32.19	5.04	5.67
Baseline: Average	48.54	4.88	6.96

5x5	MSE	L1	RMSE
XGBoost	**8.05**	**1.59**	2.83
CNN	8.46	1.63	**2.91**
LSTM	21.73	3.54	4.66
Baseline: Average	63.14	5.60	7.94

7x5	MSE	L1	RMSE
XGBoost	**8.03**	**1.59**	**2.83**
CNN	8.80	1.71	2.96
LSTM	19.10	3.47	4.37
Baseline: Average	71.50	5.94	8.45

9x5	MSE	L1	RMSE
XGBoost	**8.41**	1.65	**2.90**
CNN	8.44	**1.63**	2.92
LSTM	10.07	2.22	3.17
Baseline: Average	82.00	6.35	9.05

Evaluation Metrics and Baseline: To evaluate the accuracy of our results, we compare different methods in terms of mean L1 distance, MSE and RMSE errors on the testing data. Meanwhile, to get a better performance, we train our networks under different size of snapshot, i.e., different numbers of consecutive inflow and outflow network points and time steps. We employ the average model as the baseline method for comparison, which just simply averages the input as the prediction.

4.4   Experiment Results

For the traffic speed prediction, Table 1 shows the performances of different numbers of time steps while Table 2 indicates the results under different number of neighboring points/sensors. From Table 1, we can see, with the 4 inflow and 4 outflow consecutive points fixed, as the number of time steps increases, the performances of all methods become better in terms of MSE, L1 and RMSE errors. In addition, through the comparison, XGBoost presents more accurate and robust performance. When the input size is 9×1, CNN achieves the best performance than other methods. From Table 2, the interesting discovery is that, when the row size of snapshot is 7, i.e., 3 inflow and 3 outflow consecutive network points plus itself, XGBoost get the best performance. When the input size is 1×5, CNN achieves the best prediction.

Overall, we find that the XGBoost model shows the best performance in most cases, while the CNN model shows the second best performance. The LSTM model presents worse results than CNN and XGBoost, because we find that it is challenging to set up the hyper parameters of the LSTM model for our collected data. Through the experiments, all machine learning methods (CNN, XGBoost and LSTM) show much more accurate and robust performance than the baseline average method.

5   Conclusion

This paper presents the study of applying machine learning methods on the short-term traffic speed prediction problem. CNN is able to learn from a time-space traffic speed matrices and extracts a feature map; LSTM is able to learn time series with long time dependency; XGBoost is able to learn a decision tree model for the input vector. To validate the performance of these methods, six-month traffic speed data with the time interval of 5 minutes from 30 traffic network points/sensors were collected from the Caltrans Performance Measurement System (PeMS). The numerical experiments demonstrate that the XGBoost, CNN and LSTM outperforms the baseline average method in terms of accuracy and stability. One limitation to this study is that the advantages of neural networks, e.g., LSTM, are not fully exploited possibly because the input time-space speed matrix is not large enough and setting hyper-parameters is challenging. Future work should investigate relationship of traffic speed over the whole network and in more time steps, and propose novel neural network structures.

Acknowledgement. This research work is supported by NVIDIA GPU Grant.

References

1. Li, S., Yu, H., Zhang, J., Yang, K., Bin, R.: Video-based traffic data collection system for multiple vehicle types. IET Intell. Transport Syst. **8**(2), 164–174 (2014)

2. Song, Z., Guo, Y., Wu, Y., Ma, J.: Short-term traffic speed prediction under different data collection time intervals using a SARIMA-SDGM hybrid prediction model. PLoS One **14**(6), 1–19 (2019)
3. Liu, D., Tang, L., Shen, G., Han, X.: Traffic speed prediction: an attention-based method. Sensors **19**(18) (2019)
4. Sims, A.G., Dobinson, K.W.: The Sydney coordinated adaptive traffic (SCAT) system philosophy and benefits. IEEE Trans. Veh. Technol. **29**(2), 130–137 (1980)
5. Gartner, N., Tarnoff, P., Andrews, C.: Evaluation of optimized policies for adaptive control strategy. Transp. Res. Rec. **1324**, 105–114 (1991)
6. Gartner, N., Stamatiadis, C., Tarnoff, P.: Development of advanced traffic signal control strategies for intelligent transportation systems: multilevel design. Transp. Res. Rec. **1494**, 98–105 (1995)
7. Hunt, P., Robertson, D., Bretherton, R., Winton, R.: Scoot - a traffic responsive method of coordinating signals, TRRL LR1014, Transport and Road Research Laboratory, Crowthorne, UK (1981)
8. Chandra, S., Al-Deek, H.: Predictions of freeway traffic speeds and volumes using vector autoregressive models. J. Intell. Transpo. Syst. **13**(2), 53–72 (2009)
9. Cremer, M., Keller, H.: A new class of dynamic methods for the identification of origin-destination flows. Transp. Res. Part B Methodol. **21**(2), 117–132 (1987)
10. Ghosh, B., Basu, B., O'Mahony, M.: Bayesian time-series model for short-term traffic-flow forecasting. J. Transp. Eng. **133**(3), 180–189 (2007)
11. Dougherty, M.S., Kirby, H.R., Boyle, R.D.: The use of neural networks to recognise and predict traffic congestion. Traffic Eng. Control **34**(6) (1993)
12. Park, D., Rilett, L.R.: Forecasting multiple-period freeway link travel times using modular neural networks. Transp. Res. Rec. **1617**(1), 163–170 (1998)
13. Lingras, P., Sharma, S., Zhong, M.: Prediction of recreational travel using genetically designed regression and time-delay neural network models. Transp. Res. Rec. **1805**(1), 16–24 (2002)
14. van Lint, J.W.C., Hoogendoorn, S.P., van Zuylen, H.J.: Freeway travel time prediction with state-space neural networks: modeling state-space dynamics with recurrent neural networks. Transp. Res. Rec. **1811**(1), 30–39 (2002)
15. Zhang, W., Lee, D.-H., M. ASCE, Shi, Q.: Short-term freeway traffic flow prediction: Bayesian combined neural network approach. J. Transp. Eng. **132**(02), 114-121 (2006)
16. Long, E.S.J., Darrell, T.: Fully convolutional networks for semantic segmentation. In: IEEE Conference on Computer Vision and Pattern Recognition (CVPR) (2015)
17. Ren, S., He, K., Girshick, R., Sun, J.: Faster R-CNN: towards real-time object detection with region proposal networks. In: Advances in Neural Information Processing Systems (NIPS) (2015)
18. Lv, Y., Duan, Y., Kang, W., Li, Z., Wang, F.: Traffic flow prediction with big data: a deep learning approach. IEEE Trans. Intell. Transp. Syst. **16**(2), 865–873 (2014)
19. Li, L., Qin, L., Qu, X., Zhang, J., Wang, Y., Ran, B.: Day-ahead traffic flow forecasting based on a deep belief network optimized by the multi-objective particle swarm algorithm. Knowl.-Based Syst. **172**, 1–14 (2019)
20. Ran, X., Shan, Z., Fang, Y., Lin, C.: A convolution component-based method with attention mechanism for travel-time prediction. Sensors **19**(9) (2019)
21. Gu, Y., Lu, W., Qin, L., Li, M., Shao, Z.: Short-term prediction of lane-level traffic speeds: a fusion deep learning model. Transp. Res. Part C: Emerg. Technol. **106**, 1–16 (2019)

22. Yu, H., Wu, Z., Wang, S., Wang, Y., Ma, X.: Spatio-temporal recurrent convolutional networks for traffic prediction in transportation networks. Sensors **17**(7), 1501 (2017)
23. Fouladgar, M., Parchami, M., Elmasri, R., Ghaderi, A.: Scalable deep traffic flow neural networks for urban traffic congestion prediction. In: International Joint Conference on Neural Networks (IJCNN) (2017)
24. S. of California. Pems (2014). http://pems.dot.ca.gov/
25. Fukushima, K.: Neural network model for a mechanism of pattern recognition unaffected by shift in position - neocognitron. Trans. IECE **J62–A**(10), 658–665 (1979)
26. Chen, T., Guestrin, C.: XGBoost: a scalable tree boosting system. In: Proceedings of the 22nd ACM SIGKDD International Conference on Knowledge Discovery and Data Mining, pp. 785–794 (2016)

Intelligent Transportation

A Privacy Preserving Data Collecting Scheme in Vanet

Wang Qinglong, Tan Zhiqiang[⊠], Fan Na, and Duan Zongtao[ORCID]

School of Information Engineering, Chang'An University, Xi'an, Shaanxi, China
201424090124@chd.edu.cn

Abstract. As an important application of Vanet (Vehicle Ad hoc network), the Vehicle Crowd Sense (VCS) uses intelligent vehicles as sensing nodes to collect road information. In VCS, vehicle information is shared, which necessitates privacy protection. How to balance information sharing and privacy protection is a great challenge. Identity privacy protection is the basic requirement of VCS. In many schemes, pseudonyms are used to protect the vehicle's identity privacy. However, it is inconvenient to update and manage pseudonyms. Specifically, in our scheme, the vehicle's identity privacy is protected without pseudonyms. Furthermore, our scheme supports reputation privacy protection. Finally, security analysis shows that our scheme satisfies the requirement of privacy preserving, and the experiment and performance analysis show our scheme is efficient on computation and communication.

Keywords: Vanet · Privacy preserving · Vehicle crowd sensing · Reputation

1 Introduction

MCS(Mobile Crowd Sensing) [13,18,19] has been used for large scale sensing, with the rapid growth of holdings of mobile devices. MCS has many applications [7] in traffic monitoring, health care, other human behavior analysis and surrounding environment sensing. As its main advantages, MCS promotes the dissemination and exchange of information. In the model of MCS, the bottom layer is a sensing one composed of mobile nodes (such as mobile phones), and mobile nodes are responsible for sensing data. The middle layer is a communication network composed of base stations, responsible for communicating with mobile nodes, uploading data, and forwarding sensing results to the top layer, i.e., the collector.

In recent years, as a form of MCS, VCS (Vehicle Crowd Sense) [17] has developed rapidly. It is the technical foundation for the future scenarios like autonomous driving and collaborative sensing of vehicles and roads. Vehicles can

This work was supported in part by the Funds for Key Research and Development Plan Project of Shaanxi Province, China (No.2019ZDLGY17-08, 2018GY-136, 2018GY-022).

J. Wang et al. (Eds.): GPC 2020 Workshops, CCIS 1311, pp. 45–58, 2020.
https://doi.org/10.1007/978-981-33-4532-4_4

upload various types of sensing data [10], such as vehicle condition information, road condition information, and environmental information. These information provides data support for management agencies so that they can improve service quality, monitor road conditions and broadcast traffic incidents. More importantly, VCS can reduce the financial and time cost for data collectors, making it of more practical value.

In VCS, the vehicle communicates with RSU (Road Side Unit) to exchange information. The communication between RSU and the vehicle is achieved by insecure wireless channels. These channels could face many types of attacks, which threatens users' privacy [24]. Therefore, security and privacy have been captivating growing attention in VCS research efforts [2,15]. Li et al. [8] listed four aspects of security and privacy in VCS, including message authentication, confidentiality, integrity, and identity privacy protection. Among these, identity privacy protection is the main aspect. Many schemes use pseudonyms to implement identity privacy protection [17]. However, due to link-attack, it is possible for an attacker to link different messages from the same user, thereby threatening the user's identity privacy. For example, an attacker may reconstruct the vehicle's driving trajectory and infer other personal information such as the user's workplace and living place. So, to resist link-attack, each pseudonym can only be used for a limited time. This may cause a huge cost of managing and updating pseudonym.

Apart from the endangered user's privacy, the VCS system may also face many other types of threats. In VCS, the vehicle is not trusted, which may be malicious, performing dishonesty and sending false report [20]. The reputation-based system [1,12] is currently the most preferred method to solve this problem. Reputation is used to denote the trust level of vehicles. It is noteworthy that reputation is also a part of the vehicle's privacy, which needs to be protected [12]. Some scholars have designed the privacy preserving reputation system for MCS [12,20], which cannot be applied to VCS because the application scenarios of MCS and VCS are different. As an example, Jaimes et al. [4] designed a reputation management system for the V2V communication scenario, which is not suitable for the data collection scenario.

In this paper, we proposed a new privacy preserving data collecting scheme in Vanet. The main contributions are as follows:

1) In our scheme, the identity privacy protection of the vehicle does not involve any pseudonyms, so it avoids the complicated process of pseudonym updating and management.
2) Our scheme can better protect the vehicle's reputation privacy, that is, the vehicle will not reveal its real reputation level during the processes of data collection and reputation updating.
3) Unlike other similar schemes, where the collector is regarded as a trusted entity, our scheme treats both RSU and the collector as semi-trusted entity, which is closer to the actual situation.

2   Related Work

Many scheme have been designed for MCS to protect identity privacy. Most of them use anonymous authentication to meet the requirement. For example, Li et al. designed a privacy-preserving mobile crowd sensing scheme [7]. In this scheme, users use tokens to take part in tasks, upload data, and finally redeem rewards. It cuts the correlation between user information and realizes unlinkability. Similar, in [5], Li et al. designed an anonymous group authentication to ensure the reliability of forwarded messages through the anonymous confirmation of messages by multiple nodes.

While MCS is different from VCS, many scholars combined pseudonyms with fog computing to protect identity privacy in VCS scenarios. In [21], the researcher proposed a road condition monitoring scheme using the fog computing model. In the scheme, the vehicle uses the short-term pseudonyms and the short-term keys to communicate with RSU. These pseudonyms and keys are derived from their long-term pseudonyms and secret keys frequently, increasing the burden of TA. Also, fog computing model can be used to design a privacy-preserving traffic monitoring system [22]. In these schemes [21,22], RSU, as the edge of the network, completes the functions of message identification and false report filtering. Similarly, Li et al. [6] designed a privacy-preserving traffic monitoring system for VCS, which also uses the pseudonym. However, Zhu et al. [23] pointed out that the pseudonym is vulnerable to differential attacks. The vehicle could be identified even if the pseudonym is used. To avoid this problem, Shao et al. [14] designed a new group signature mechanism in Vanet to complete threshold authentication and efficient tracking without a pseudonym. But, verification and transmission cost of the group signature is much higher than that of the traditional signature.

In addition, the reputation is also a highly followed research topic in MCS and VCS. Alamri et al. [1] proposed a privacy preserving reputation system in MCS, it uses a central entity, an App server, to manage the reputation of mobile nodes. In VCS, Jaimes et al. [4] designed an anonymous reputation system for V2V message forward scenarios. This scheme uses the anonymous reputation to protect the reputation privacy of the vehicles. And Oluoch et al. [11] also presented a distributed reputation scheme for V2V message forward scenarios in Vanet.

Apart from their respective contributions to privacy preservation, all schemes above are not suitable for data collection scenarios. Hence, a new scheme is suggested in the present study.

3   System Overview

In this section, we show the system model, attack model and security goal of our proposed scheme.

3.1　System Model

The system model is illustrated in Fig. 1.

1) TA: It is responsible for initializing the entire system, generating public parameters, completing registration and certification of vehicles and RSU, and responsible for generating and updating the vehicle reputation levels. We assume that the TA is completely trusted, and the TA communicates with other entities through a secure channel.

2) RSU: It is responsible for message forwarding between the vehicle and the collector, and completing anonymous authentication of the vehicle. We assume that RSU is a semi-trusted entity, that is, the RSU can honestly execute the protocol process, but it is curious about the privacy of vehicles and has the motivation to get the privacy information of the vehicle. At the same time, we assume that RSU communicates with the vehicle and the collector through an insecure channel.

3) Vehicle: It is responsible for sensing data and submitting results to collectors. We assume that vehicle communicates with the RSU through an insecure channel, and the vehicle is an untrustworthy entity, which means that there are some malicious vehicles that perform replay, impersonation, forgery and other attacks on the information transmitted through the insecure channel.

4) Collector: It is responsible for collecting, storing and evaluating the data submitted by the vehicle. Our scheme assumes that the collector is a semi-trusted entity and communicates with the RSU through an insecure channel.

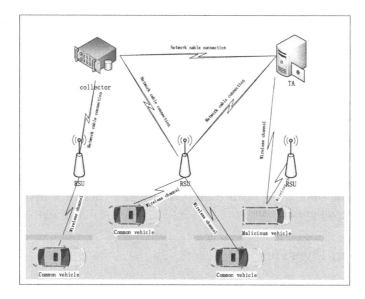

Fig. 1. system model

3.2 Attack Model

1) Replay attack: An attacker resubmits sensing data that has been previously received by the collector.
2) Impersonation attack: An attacker imitates the legal vehicle to send false messages to make a profit and offer convenience to itself. For example, an attacker could imitate an ambulance to acquire a green channel in the traffic jam.
3) Forgery attack: An attacker forges a legal message with a wrong identity.

3.3 Security Goal

1) Anonymity: Except TA, any other entities learn nothing about the identity of a vehicle from a message sent by this vehicle.
2) Unlinkability: The attacker cannot link received messages sent from the same sender.
3) Reputation privacy: Vehicles can take part in tasks without revealing their true reputation level.
4) Security: Data reported by the vehicle should be securely transmitted to prevent unauthorized entities from obtaining the reported data information.

4 Preliminaries

A bilinear map (bilinear pairing) used in this paper is defined as follows: Let G_1, G_T be cyclic groups of prime order q. Let g denote a generator of G_1, respectively. The bilinear map $e\,(g,\ g) : \ G_1 \times G_1 \to G_T$ is an efficiently computable function, satisfying the following properties:

1. Non-degeneracy: $e\,(g,\ g) \neq 1$
2. Bilinearity: $e\left(g^a,\ g^b\right) = e(g,\ g)^{ab}$ for all $a, b \in Z_q$

5 Propose Scheme

In this section, we proposed a privacy preserving data collecting scheme in Vanet. Our scheme can be divided into the following parts: system initialization, data submission, reputation token generation, and reputation update. Through these steps, collectors can collect the data from vehicles without revealing the privacy of vehicles. At the same time, vehicle can update its reputation dynamically after finishing a task.

Table 1. notation

Parameter name	Description
pk_{TA}, sk_{TA}	Public and secret key of TA
pk_i, sk_i	Public and secret key of RSU_i
$cert_i, cert_c$	Certificate of RSU_i and $collector$
$HMAC_k$	Hash-MAC algorithm with key k
$e(g, g)$	Bilinear pair operation
α, β, σ	Signature of the message
pk_c, sk_c	The public key and private key of collector
PKE_{pk_c}	Asymmetric encryption the public key of collector
E_k, D_k	Symmetric encryption and decryption with key k
k_{tc}	Shared key between TA and collector

5.1 System Initialization

1) TA initialization: TA generates bilinear parameters and randomly selects $\theta, a_i \in \mathbb{Z}_q{}^*, 1 \le i \le n$ as the system master-key. g is the primitive element whose order of the multiplication group G is q, making it difficult to calculate the discrete logarithm with g as the base. Let $u_i = g^{a_i}$, $1 \le i \le n$, $g_\theta = g^\theta$. $HMAC_k(x)$ is a secure message authentication code algorithm with a key, H is a collision resistant hash function, E is a symmetric encryption algorithm, and D is a corresponding symmetric decryption algorithm. PKE is an asymmetric algorithm. $e(g, g)$ is a bilinear map. The public key and private key of TA is pk_{TA} and sk_{TA}, respectively. TA keeps $< a_i, \theta, sk_{TA} >$ secret. The system parameters $< G, G_T, g, e, q, g_\theta, u_i, HMAC, H, e(g, g), E, D, PKE >$ are disclosed, and the public parameters are stored in the vehicle's equipment and RSU in advance.

2) Vehicle initialization: before the vehicle enters the network, it must register the relevant information on the TA. During the registration, the vehicle needs to provide its real identity ID_i to TA (such as license plate number, user ID number, etc.). If identity is verified, TA will select secret key randomly $x_{i1}, x_{i2}, ..., x_{in} \in \mathbb{Z}_q{}^*$, compute $\sum_{j=1}^{n} a_j x_{ij} = s_i$, $y_i' = g^{\frac{1}{\theta + s_i}}$, $g_i = g^{s_i}$. TA adds $ID_i \| s_i$ into the Trace List TL (if s_i is equal to the stored value in TL, reselect $x_{i1}, ..., x_{in}, y_i', g_i$). Then TA sends $x_{i1}, ..., x_{in}, y_i', g_i$ to the vehicle over a secure channel as the vehicle's private key.

3) RSU initialization: for a newly added RSU_i, TA randomly generates a key pair (sk_i, pk_i) and the corresponding certificate $cert_i = pk_i \| sig(sk_{TA}; pk_i)$, and sends $cert_i \| sk_i \| pk_i$ to RSU_i.

4) Collector initialization: TA generates a key pair (sk_c, pk_c) and corresponding certificate $cert_c = pk_c \| sig(sk_{TA}; pk_c)$ for $collector$, and sends $cert_c \| sk_c \| pk_c$ to the collector.

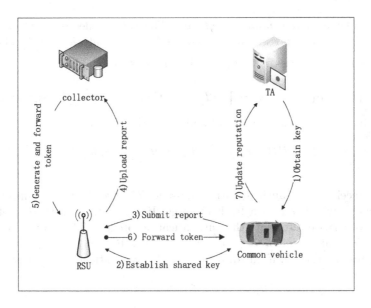

Fig. 2. system process

All necessary notations are listed in Table. 1, and system process is demonstrated in Fig. 2.

5.2 Data Submission

In the Vanet crowd sensing system, the vehicle submits data to the data collector through RSU. When RSU receives the data reported by the vehicle, it needs to verify the legal identity of the vehicle anonymously, that is, the vehicle must prove that it belongs to the legal vehicles in the system without revealing its real identity. The process are as follows:

1) RSU periodically broadcasts the authentication message. Before broadcasting a new authentication message, RSU_i randomly selects $R \in \mathbb{Z}_q^*$ and calculates $T_i = (u_i)^R$, $1 \le i \le n$, $T_\theta = (g_\theta)^R$. Then RSU_i broadcasts the current message $Auth^{(RSU_i)} = M||T_\theta||\sigma||cert_i||tl$, where $M = T_1||T_2||...||T_n$, $\sigma = sig(sk_i; M||T_\theta)$ and tl means task level.

2) When the vehicle newly enters the RSU_i communication area, it will receive the currently broadcasted authentication message $Auth^{(RSU_i)}$, and then, vehicle verifies whether both the $cert_i$ and signature σ are valid or not. If either one is invalid, terminate the process.

3) Let the data generated by the vehicle be *report*, and the vehicle encrypts the data $W = PKE_{pk_c}(report||grade||time)$ with the public key pk_c of the collector, where *grade* represents the reputation level of the vehicle. In this scheme, the reputation level of the vehicle is classified into

four ranks, i.e., $low, middle, high, top$. The data collector can select special vehicles, who possess designated or higher reputation level. The vehicle randomly chooses $r \in \mathbb{Z}_q^*$, and computes $c_1 = \prod_{j=1}^{n} (u_j)^{r x_{ij}}$, $c_2 = (y_i')^{\frac{1}{r}}$,
$c_3 = (T_\theta)^r$, $c_4 = g^r$, $k = \prod_{j=1}^{n} (T_j)^{r x_{ij}}$, then computes the signature $\beta = HMAC_k (c_1||c_2||c_3||c_4||W||time)$ and sends the report

$$RP = c_1||c_2||c_3||c_4||W||time||grade||\beta$$

4) Upon receiving the authentication message RP, use the time stamp $time$ to determine whether it is a fresh message. If so, continue with the following steps, otherwise terminate the authentication process. Then RSU_i computes validation parameters $k' = (c_1)^R$ and $\beta' = HMAC_{k'} (c_1||c_2||c_3||c_4||time)$ and validates the Eq. (1), if failed, terminate the authentication process:

$$\beta = \beta' \tag{1}$$

Then RSU_i then verifies Eq. (2) (3) are established:

$$e(g_\theta, c_4) = e(g, c_3') \tag{2}$$

$$e(c_2, c_1 c_3') = e(g, g) \tag{3}$$

if established, RSU_i will compute signature $\sigma_2 = sig(sk_i; c_4||W)$ and send $RP' = c_4||W||\sigma_2$ to the collector.

5.3 Reputation Token Generation

When receives the RP' from RSU_i, the collector will carry out the following process:

1) The collector checks whether the signature σ_2 is valid or not by the public key of RSU_i. If so, continue, otherwise discard the message.
2) The collector uses its secret key to decrypt W and obtains $report||grade||time$. The collector judges whether the report is fresh according to $time$, if so, continue, otherwise discard the message.
3) The collector checks whether the grade level $grade$ meets the requirements. If so, use the public key of the TA pk_{TA} to verify whether the contained signature is valid. If so, then it will accept the data in the report. After the collector receives the data, it judges the quality of the data and then generates a reputation level $level_i$ for the report. Then the collector encrypts $level_i$ by the shared key k_{tc} and gains $T_i = E_{k_{tc}} (level_i||time)$. The collector randomly selects $R_c \in \mathbb{Z}_q^*$ and computes $k_2 = (c_4)^{R_c}$, then generates $token = (g^{R_c}||T_i||time||\alpha)$, and $\alpha = HMAC_{k_2} (g^{R_c}||T_i||time)$. Once the collector sends $X_2 = E_{k_2} (token||\alpha)$ to RSU_i, RSU_i will forward it to the vehicle.

4) After receiving X_2, the vehicle verifies it by following steps: determines if the *time* in the token is fresh, if not discard the message, otherwise compute $k_2' = \left(g^{R_c}\right)^r$ and $\alpha' = HMAC_{k_2}\left(g^{R_c}||T_i||time\right)$, verify whether $\alpha = \alpha'$ is established or not, if so, accept T_i.

5.4 Reputation Update

After the data collection task is accomplished, the vehicle can initiate a reputation update request to the TA, as follows:

1) The vehicle sends $req = ID_i||T_1||T_2||...||T_n$ to the TA through a secure channel, where T_i represents all the reputation ratings the vehicle obtained during this task. Here, the reputation rating is encrypted, and the vehicle cannot know the specific rate level in each reputation rating. Thus, all T_i will be provided to the TA, preventing the vehicle from only providing TA with the reputation ratings that are beneficial to its rating, excluding the bad ones.

2) After receiving the request from the vehicle, TA uses the key k_{tc} shared with the collector to decrypt all the reputation ratings T_i and verifies that they are in a valid period. TA uses all valid reputation rating information to update the vehicle's current reputation level $level_i$. Assuming the reputation level of the vehicle is updated from previous level *middle* to *high*. TA generates the corresponding reputation levels separately $grade_h = high||time||\sigma$, $grade_m = middle||time||\sigma$, and $grade_l = low||time||\sigma$, where σ represents the signature of TA, finally TA sends $grade_h, grade_m, grade_l$ to the vehicle through an secure channel. Here, grade *high* is the highest grade that the vehicle owns currently. In our scheme, we define the highest reputation level as the true reputation level of the vehicle.

6 Security Analysis

In this section, we show that our scheme can achieve the security goal in Sect. 3.1 and resist the attack we listed in Sect. 3.2.

6.1 Attack Analysis

1) Replay attack: The messages sent by all entities in the scheme contain time stamp information, so they can resist replay attack.

2) Impersonation attack: The attacker cannot achieve the purpose of the impersonation attack by tampering with the intercepted legitimate messages. It means that the only way an attacker successfully implements the impersonation attack is to obtain the private key of a legitimate vehicle. Since the private key is assumed secure in our scheme, it means our scheme can resist impersonation attack.

3) Forgery attack: According to the scheme construction, if the attacker wants to achieve the purpose of forgery attack, it means that he must successfully forge a valid private key $x_{i1}, ..., x_{in}, y_i', g_i$. Here the attacker can choose $x_{i1}, ..., x_{in}, y_i', g_i \in \mathbb{Z}_q^*$, and compute $g_i = \prod_{j=1}^{n} (u_j)^{x_{ij}} = g^s$. But from the security assumptions [3], even if the attacker knows $< g, g^\theta, g^s >$, it can not get $g^{\frac{1}{\theta+s}}$. It means, the attacker cannot obtain y_i' in the private key, that is, the attacker cannot forge a valid private key. Thus, our scheme can resist forgery attack.

6.2   Security Goal Analysis

1) Anonymity: According to the scheme, the data reported by the vehicle does not contain the true identity information of the vehicle. Neither the malicious attacker nor the RSU or the collector can obtain the true identity of the vehicle, that is, the scheme satisfies anonymity.
2) Unlinkability: Because the vehicle selects a different random number each time a message is reported, neither the attacker nor the RSU or the collector can link different messages reported by the same vehicle, indicating that the scheme satisfies unlinkability.
3) Reputation privacy: When the vehicle participates in the data collection task if the required reputation level is not higher than the highest level it owns, the vehicle is eligible to participate in the task. In order not to reveal the privacy of the vehicles reputation level, the vehicle only needs to show the reputation level required by the task when submitting data, instead of its true reputation level, thereby protecting the reputation privacy of the vehicle. Besides, from the perspective of the collector, the data reported by all vehicles participating in the same task contain the same reputation level, so it is impossible to use the reputation level to carry out link attack. Hence, the reputation privacy of the vehicle is better protected.
4) Security: Data collected by the vehicle are encrypted with the public key of the collector, so neither the attacker nor the RSU can obtain the actual content of the data reported by the vehicle, that is, our scheme satisfies security.

Table 2. Security comparison

Security	[16]	Ours
Message authentication	✓	✓
Identity privacy preserving	✓	✓
Unlinkability	×	✓
Resistance to replay attack	✓	✓
Resistance to impersonation attack	✓	✓
Resistance to modification attack	✓	✓

In terms of security, we compared our scheme with another similar scheme [16] which was published very recently and listed the results in Table 2. In [16], Wang et al. designed a source authentication scheme for road condition monitoring without pseudonym. The main shortage of [16] is that it dose not satisfy unlinkability, while our scheme does. Further, Wang does not consider the reputation of vehicles.

7   Performance Analysis

In this section, we implement our scheme and analyze the computational and communication cost. We compare our scheme with [16], which proves our scheme has a better computational cost.

Table 3. Operation time cost

Operation	Description	Computational cost
T_{pair}	Pairing operation	5.59 ms
T_{exp}	Exponential operation	0.68 ms
T_{mul}	Multiplication operation	0.91 ms
T_{ECC}	ECC encryption operation	1.43 ms
T_{HMAC}	HMAC operation	1.3 ms

Table 4. Time cost comparison

Item	[16]	Ours
Steps carried out by vehicle	$11 \times T_{exp} + 2 \times T_{pair} = 18.66$ ms	$5 \times T_{exp} + 6 \times T_{mul} = 8.86$ ms
Steps carried out by RSU	$7 \times T_{exp} + 4 \times T_{pair} = 27.12$ ms	$5 \times T_{exp} + 4 \times T_{pair} = 25.76$ ms

7.1   Computational Cost

The calculation performance of the scheme in this paper mainly depends on the exponential operation and bilinear pairing operation. For the proposed scheme, we use a type A bilinear pairing [9], and Advanced Encryption Standard (AES) as the symmetric encryption algorithm, Elliptic Curve Cryptography (ECC) as the asymmetric encryption algorithm and the hash algorithm is SHA1. The experimental environment is Intel (R) Core (TM) i7-6700 3.4-GHz machine with

16-GB memory, the JAVA version is 1.8.0-131, JPBC uses default parameters. According to the proposed scheme, time cost to generate an RSU authentication message is $T_{Auth_{RSU}} = 5 \times T_{exp}$, to generate a vehicle report is $T_{Report_{Veh}} = 8 \times T_{exp} + 6 \times T_{mul} + T_{ECC}$, and to verify a vehicle authentication message by RSU is $T_{Verify_{RSU}} = 4 \times T_{pair}$. We measured the time taken for the basic operation, which is shown in Table 3.

And we compare the time cost of the steps carried out by a vehicle and RSU with [16] in Table 4. It can be shown by comparison that our scheme has a less computational cost.

7.2   Communication Cost

The communication overhead is the size of transmitting messages. In the proposed scheme, one authentication message of RSU, consists of $\{M||T_\theta|| \sigma||cert_i||tl\}$, where $M = T_1||T_2||...||T_n$, $\sigma = sig\,(sk_i; M||T_\theta)$, M is a $n \times 512$ bits variable, T_θ is also 512 bits, and we set $n = 3$. σ is 224-bits, $cert_i$ is 32 bits, and tl is 4 bits. So the total communication overhead of one RSU authentication message is 356 bytes. Besides, one vehicle's report message, consists of $c_1||c_2||c_3||c_4||time||W||\beta$, where c_i is a 512 bits variable. $time$ is 32 bits, and W is 256 bits. And the total communication overhead of one vehicle report message is 320 bytes. The reputation token sent by the collector consists of $X_2 = token||\alpha$ and $token = (g^{R_c}||T_i||time||\alpha)$ where g^{R_c} and T_i is 512 bits, and α is same as β. So the total communication overhead of reputation token message is 140 bytes. Because the vehicle reporting process is a common part, we compared the communication cost of RSU's authentication message and the vehicle's report with [16]. Results are demonstrated in Table 5. Since in our scheme, vehicle's sensing data was submitted to the data collector through RSU, while in [16], vehicle direct report the data to data collector, there was a higher communication cost on RSU's authentication message when compared to [16]. But, there was a lower communication cost on the vehicles report in our scheme.

Table 5. Communication cost comparison

Communication cost	[16]	Ours
RSU's authentication message	180 bytes	320 bytes
Vehicle's report	440 bytes	356 bytes

8   Conclusion

This paper proposed a privacy preserving data collection scheme in Vanet with two notable contributions. First, in our scheme, mutual anonymous authentication is designed to protect the identity of the vehicle which can resist link attack from the RSU and the collector. Second, the actual reputation level of the vehicle is not revealed during the process of data collection and reputation updating, so the reputation privacy is preserved, and the data is transmitted securely by encryption. Security analysis proved that the scheme satisfied anonymity, unlinkability, reputation privacy, and security. Experiment showed that the scheme had lower computational overhead and communication overhead.

References

1. Alamri, B.H., Monowar, M.M., Alshehri, S.: A privacy-preserving collaborative reputation system for mobile crowdsensing. Int. J. Distrib. Sens. Netw. (2018)
2. Basudan, S., Lin, X., Sankaranarayanan, K.: A privacy-preserving vehicular crowdsensing-based road surface condition monitoring system using fog computing. IEEE Internet Things J. **4**(3), 772–782 (2017)
3. Boneh, D., Boyen, X.: Short signatures without random oracles. In: Cachin, C., Camenisch, J.L. (eds.) EUROCRYPT 2004. LNCS, vol. 3027, pp. 56–73. Springer, Heidelberg (2004). https://doi.org/10.1007/978-3-540-24676-3_4
4. Jaimes, L.M.S., Ullah, K., dos Santos Moreira, E.: ARS: anonymous reputation system for vehicular ad hoc networks. In: 2016 8th IEEE Latin-American Conference on Communications (LATINCOM), pp. 1–6, November 2016
5. Li, L., et al.: CreditCoin: a privacy-preserving blockchain-based incentive announcement network for communications of smart vehicles. IEEE Trans. Intell. Transp. Syst. **19**(7), 2204–2220 (2018)
6. Li, M., Zhu, L., Lin, X.: Privacy-preserving traffic monitoring with false report filtering via fog-assisted vehicular crowdsensing. IEEE Trans. Serv. Comput. (2019)
7. Li, Q., Cao, G.: Providing privacy-aware incentives in mobile sensing systems. IEEE Trans. Mob. Comput. **15**(6), 1485–1498 (2016)
8. Li, W., Song, H.: ART: an attack-resistant trust management scheme for securing vehicular ad hoc networks. IEEE Trans. Intell. Transp. Syst. **17**(4), 960–969 (2016)
9. Lipmaa, H.: Pairing-based cryptography, vol. 22, no. 3, pp. 573–590 (2005)
10. Ni, J., Zhang, A., Lin, X., Shen, X.S.: Security, privacy, and fairness in fog-based vehicular crowdsensing. IEEE Commun. Mag. **55**(6), 146–152 (2017)
11. Oluoch, J.: A distributed reputation scheme for situation awareness in vehicular ad hoc networks (VANETs). In: 2016 IEEE International Multi-Disciplinary Conference on Cognitive Methods in Situation Awareness and Decision Support (CogSIMA), pp. 63–67, March 2016
12. Primiero, G., Martorana, A., Tagliabue, J.: Simulation of a trust and reputation based mitigation protocol for a black hole style attack on VANETs. In: 2018 IEEE European Symposium on Security and Privacy Workshops (EuroS PW), pp. 127–135, April 2018
13. Ray, A., Mallick, S., Mondal, S., Paul, S., Chowdhury, C., Roy, S.: A framework for mobile crowd sensing and computing based systems. In: 2018 IEEE International Conference on Advanced Networks and Telecommunications Systems (ANTS), pp. 1–6, December 2018
14. Shao, J., Lin, X., Lu, R., Zuo, C.: A threshold anonymous authentication protocol for VANETs. IEEE Trans. Veh. Technol. **65**(3), 1711–1720 (2016)
15. Vergara-Laurens, I.J., Jaimes, L.G., Labrador, M.A.: Privacy-preserving mechanisms for crowdsensing: survey and research challenges. IEEE Internet Things J. **4**(4), 855–869 (2017)

16. Wang, Y., Ding, Y., Wu, Q., Wei, Y., Qin, B., Wang, H.: Privacy-preserving cloud-based road condition monitoring with source authentication in VANETs. IEEE Trans. Inf. Forensics Secur. **14**(7), 1779–1790 (2019)

17. Wei, J., Xiaojie, W., Nan, L., Guomin, Y., Yi, M.: A privacy-preserving fog computing framework for vehicular crowdsensing networks. IEEE Access (2019)

18. Yang, D., Xue, G., Fang, X., Tang, J.: Crowdsourcing to smartphones: incentive mechanism design for mobile phone sensing (2012)

19. Yao, W., Wu, Y., Zeng, J., Hong, C., Li, C.: PIE: a personalized incentive for location-aware mobile crowd sensing. In: 2017 IEEE Symposium on Computers and Communications (ISCC) (2017)

20. Yao, X., Zhang, X., Ning, H., Li, P.: Using trust model to ensure reliable data acquisition in VANETs. Ad Hoc Netw. **55**, 107–118 (2017)

21. Zhang, L., Hu, C., Wu, Q., Domingo-Ferrer, J., Qin, B.: Privacy-preserving vehicular communication authentication with hierarchical aggregation and fast response. IEEE Trans. Comput. **65**(8), 2562–2574 (2016)

22. Zhu, L., Li, M., Zhang, Z.: Secure fog-assisted crowdsensing with collusion resistance: from data reporting to data requesting. IEEE Internet Things J. **6**, 5473–5484 (2019)

23. Zhu, T., Li, G., Zhou, W., Yu, P.S.: Differentially private data publishing and analysis: a survey. IEEE Trans. Knowl. Data Eng. **29**(8), 1619–1638 (2017)

24. Zhu, X., Samadh, S.A., Yu, T.: Large scale active vehicular crowdsensing. In: 2018 IEEE 88th Vehicular Technology Conference (VTC-Fall), pp. 1–5, August 2018

An Experimental Method for CAV Dedicated Lane Setting Strategy

Hongge Zhu[1(✉)], Xiaodong Zhu[1], Zhigang Xu[2], Bin Tian[2], and Yuqin Zhang[2]

[1] China Highway Engineering Consultants Corporation, Beijing 100000, China
allen.phd@139.com, zxd7612@hotmail.com
[2] Chang'an University, Xi'an 710064, China
{xuzhigang,tb}@chd.edu.cn

Abstract. With the implement of Intelligent Vehicle Infrastructure System (IVIS) and automated driving, the requirement of setting a Connected Automated Vehicle (CAV) dedicated lane in highway is increased. However, the penetration of CAVs is low at the beginning of this application, and it will increase gradually in the future. Therefore, it is necessary to investigate the setting strategy of the CAV dedicated lane. Here, an experimental method is proposed to set the CAV dedicated lane dynamically according to the traffic flow and the penetration of CAVs. The performance has been evaluated by using Plexe that is a platoon simulation platform. Simulation results show that the proposed method improves traffic flow 25.3% compared with the benchmark method.

Keywords: Dedicated lane · CAV · HDV · Mixed traffic flow

1 Introduction

With the development of Connected Automated Vehicles (CAVs), it is generally expected that an early stage CAVs will exist in the heterogeneous traffic flow. Currently, it can be confirmed that CAVs will be allowed to drive on certain highway section. Maybe the application could start at commercial vehicles that is controlled like Connected Vehicles (CVs). For a CV, the vehicle still be operated by a driver but the driver will follow the commends on a console. Nevertheless, the era of automated vehicles will arrive eventually. Consequently, the lanes deployment dedicated for CAVs has become a critical issue.

In 2017, China Highway Engineering Consultants Corporation (CHECC) started to design the Intelligent Vehicle Infrastructure System (IVIS) for "Yancong" Highway (Beijing section) that is a main connection road line of 2022 Winter Olympics [1]. CAVs Dedicated lane is considered to set in the highway. However, the penetration rate of CAVs is related to both the technical and the politic issues. Objectively, the CAV dedicated lanes will reduce the number of lanes for other conventional vehicles. Traffic flow could be influenced greatly if the CAV dedicated lanes cannot be set properly. Therefore, a setting method of CAVs dedicated lanes is worth to investigate.

© Springer Nature Singapore Pte Ltd. 2020
J. Wang et al. (Eds.): GPC 2020 Workshops, CCIS 1311, pp. 59–66, 2020.
https://doi.org/10.1007/978-981-33-4532-4_5

We believe that there is a certain threshold of CAVs penetration, beyond which the traffic flow will be improve by setting a CAV lane. Moreover, with the increasing of the CAVs penetration, only one CAVs dedicated lane could be not enough. However, the impact of CAV dedicated lane on traffic flow is a complex problem. It involves not only the CAVs penetration rate but also the performance of the CAVs compared to regular vehicles.

Therefore, this paper uses an experimental method to discuss the impact of CAV dedicated lane on the traffic flow, and proposes a straightforward strategy to set CAV dedicated lane adaptively.

2   Related Work

There is the literature on the impact of adaptive cruise control vehicles on traffic flow. Ioannou and Chien developed an autonomous intelligent cruise control system and found that the developed system contributes to a faster and smoother traffic flow [2]. Arem et al. studied the impact of a cooperative ACC (CACC) on the traffic-flow characteristics and found that the traffic-flow stability can be improved along with a slight increase in the flow efficiency [4]. Kesting et al. employed an ACC strategy to improve traffic stability and increase dynamic road capacity [5]. At the roadway level, Chen et al. also developed a mathematical framework for the optimal deployment of autonomous vehicle lanes in a road network [8]. Chen et al. proposed a set of capacity formulation which takes into consideration the AV penetration rate, micro/mesoscopic characteristic and different lane policies for accommodating AVs [9]. Ghiasi et al. proposed an analytical capacity model and lane management model of the mixed traffic using a Markov chain method [10].

Simulation is an effective approach that can be utilized to investigate this problem. Talebpour et al. investigated the effects of reserved lanes for AVs on congestion and travel time reliability [11]. In their work, three different strategies were assessed and compared, it found that optional use of the CAV dedicated lane for CAVs can ease congestion and has better performance over other policies. Using monte carlo simulations, Kakimoto found that as the proportion of self-driving cars increased, safety, efficiency and comfort improved [12]. Mardesden et al. studied the potential impacts of adaptive cruise control (ACC) on motorway driving via microscopic simulation [3]. Shladover et al. estimated the impact of ACC and CACC vehicles on highway capacity under different market penetration rates through micro-simulation, and found that when the market penetration rate reached a medium-high percentage, adaptive cruise control vehicles could significantly improve capacity [6]. Talebpour and Mahmassani presented a simulation framework using different models with some technology-appropriate assumptions to study the influence of CAVs on traffic flow stability and throughput [7].

3   Scenario Formulation

3.1   Human-Driven Vehicles (HDV)

The Krauss car-following model is selected to describe the following behavior of HDVs.

In a discrete time-step model, braking is modeled by subtracting in each time step one unit of the deceleration b from the velocity. The braking distance of the first car is then given by

$$d_p = b[(\alpha_p + \beta_p - 1) + (\alpha_p + \beta_p - 2) + \cdots + \beta_p] = b\left(\alpha_p \beta_p + \frac{\alpha_p(\alpha_p - 1)}{2}\right) \quad (1)$$

where α_p and β_p are defined as the integer and the fractional part of v_b/b, d_p is minimum braking distance, Similarly, if the second driver chooses the velocity $v_{safe} = b(\alpha_{safe} + \beta_{safe})$, his breaking distance becomes

$$d_s = b[(\alpha_{safe} + \beta_{safe}) + (\alpha_{safe} + \beta_{safe} - 1) + \cdots + \beta_{safe}]$$
$$= b\left((\alpha_{safe} + 1)\beta_{safe} + \frac{\alpha_{safe}(\alpha_{safe} - 1)}{2}\right) \quad (2)$$

If the expression is inserted into the safety condition, the resulting equation can be solved formally for α_{safe} to give

$$\alpha_{safe} = f(\beta_{safe}) \quad (3)$$

where the function $f(\beta)$ is given by

$$f(\beta) = \sqrt{2\frac{d_p + gap}{b} + \left(\beta - \frac{1}{2}\right)^2} - \left(\beta + \frac{1}{2}\right) \quad (4)$$

We know that α_{safe} is a non-negative integer and β_{safe} a non-negative real number smaller than 1. So the fact that $f(\beta)$ is a decreasing function of β and $f(0) - f(1) = 1$ immediately yields $\alpha_{safe} = [f(0)]$.

3.2 Connected Automated Vehicles (CAV)

The CTG controller car-following model were used to describe the car-following behavior of CAVs. The control law without communication delay as follows:

$$u_i = k_a \cdot a_{i-1}(t) + k_v \cdot [v_{i-1}(t) - v_i(t)] + k_s \cdot [d_i(t) - v_i(t)t_d - G_{min}] \quad (5)$$

where k_a is the gain of the preceding vehicle's acceleration, k_v is the gain of the speed difference between the following vehicle i and the preceding vehicle i−1, k_s is the gain of the spacing difference between the following vehicle i and the preceding vehicle i−1, $d_i(t)$ is the gap between the following vehicle i and the preceding vehicle i−1, G_{min} is a standstill distance, and t_d is the time headway defined in the CTG policy.

4 Experimental Method

In order to study the influence of different CAV permeability on road traffic flow under the condition of setting a CAV dedicated lane, we conducted a series of simulations based on the Plexe platform. Plexe has realistic vehicle dynamics and several cruise control models, allowing for analysis of control systems, large-scale and hybrid scenarios, as well as network protocols and cooperative maneuvers. Plexe is actually an extension of a program called Veins, which is a framework for simulating a vehicle network. Veins relies on two simulators, namely, OMNET++, an event-based network simulator, and SUMO, a road traffic simulator. Veins provides a python program that associates OMNET++ and SUMO through a TCP socket connection, thereby expanding them and providing a comprehensive set of models for inter-vehicle communication simulation.

Fig. 1. SUMO traffic model

The topology used in all experiments in this paper is shown in Fig. 1. Our simulations used Plexe 2.1 (based on Veins 4.7), OMNeT++ 5.1.1, and SUMO 0.32.0. Both the MAC layer and the physical layer of DSRC are based on the IEEE 802.11p standard. The data rate is set to the maximum broadcast rate (6 Mbit/s in IEEE 802.11p), the transmission power is set to 100 mW, and the receiver sensitivity is set to −94 dBm. The Friis free space path loss propagation model was used, in which the exponent α was assigned a value of 2.0. The size of the beacon was set to 200 bytes and the sending period of the beacon was 0.1 s. 140 vehicles are placed in a one-way three-lane road. The time headway of CAV is 0.5 s, the distance at standstill is set to 2 m and vehicle length is 4 m. The upper limit of vehicle acceleration is 2.5 m/s^2, and the minimum acceleration is − 9.0 m/s^2. The standstill distance is set to 2 m. The k_a, k_v and k_s in Eq. (5) are set to 0.6, 0.4 and 0.2. In addition, the minimum acceleration of HDV is −6 m/s^2. All simulation settings are summarized in Table 1.

In this paper, we set a CAV dedicated lane in the one-way three-lane scenario to research the traffic flow of the road with different permeability. The vehicle travels at a constant speed of 100 km/h for 120 s. The flow is measured by the induction loop and the permeability of CAV will be changed. The selected permeability values were 0%, 10%, 20%, 30%, 40%, 50%, 60%, 70%, 80%, 90% and 100%. In order to ensure the statistical accuracy of the results, we conducted several tests. The simulation results show that when a CAV dedicated lane is set, either under high CAV permeability or low CAV permeability, the traffic flow is not ideal (see Fig. 2). In the case of low CAV permeability, there will be such situation that the lanes of HDV are jammed and the lane of CAV is spare. In the case of high CAV permeability, the lanes of HDV are spare and the lane of CAV is jammed. That is to say, when CAV permeability and CAV dedicated lane settings do not match, it will cause a waste of resources and reduce the traffic flow. In this experiment,the average traffic flow is only 3000. So we propose a method to dynamically set the CAV dedicated lane.

Table 1. Simulation settings.

Item	Index	Value
Physical layer	Frequency band	5.89 GHz
	Bandwidth	10 MHz
	Tx power	100 mW
	Receiver sensitivity	−94 dBm
	FSPL exponent α	2.0
	Thermal noise	−95 dBm
Link layer	Bit rate	6 Mbit/s
	CW	[15, 1023]
	Slot time	13 μs
	SIFS	32 μs
	DIFS	58 μs
Beaconing	Beacon frequency	0.1 Hz
	Beacon size	200 bytes
Platoon system	τ	0.5 s
	t_d	0.5 s
CACC gap controller	k_a	0.6
	k_v	0.4
	k_s	0.2
	G_{min}	2 m

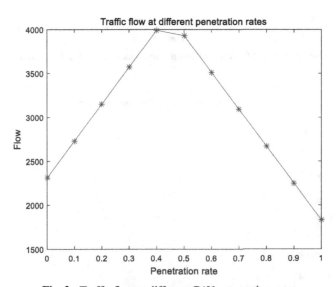

Fig. 2. Traffic flow at different CAV penetration rates

For this reason, we proposed that under the condition of low CAV permeability, no CAV dedicated lane should be set, and under the condition of high CAV permeability,

CAV dedicated lanes should be set to increase road traffic flow. However, what percentage of the CAV is low permeability and what percentage of the CAV is high permeability. Then, we researched the threshold. The experimental results show that it is reasonable to set a CAV dedicated lane when the CAV permeability is 30%–50%; when the CAV permeability is lower than 30%, no CAV dedicated lane can guarantee the maximum traffic flow; when the CAV permeability is higher than 50%, two CAV dedicated lanes can guarantee the maximum traffic flow (see Fig. 3). The average traffic increased to 3760, a 25.3% increase over the previous method.

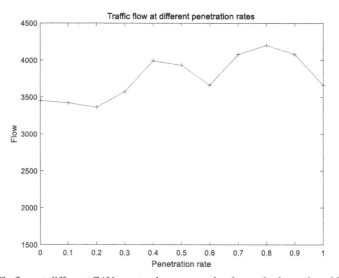

Fig. 3. Traffic flow at different CAV penetration rates under the method mentioned in the article

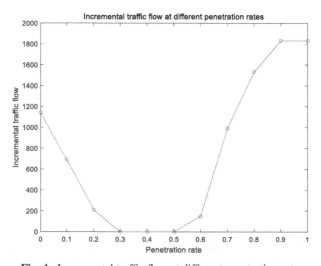

Fig. 4. Incremental traffic flow at different penetration rates

By comparison, it is found that the method of dynamic management of CAV dedicated lane can double the traffic flow in the best case and maintain a high traffic flow in the worst case (see Fig. 4). The average flow increased by 25.3%. This is of great significance to improve the efficiency of road traffic and promote the landing of CAV.

5   Conclusion

This paper studied the traffic flow under different CAV penetration rates, and conducts simulation experiments through Plexe platforms. The two CAV dedicated lane setting methods were compared, and the results show that dynamically adjusting the CAV dedicated lane, that is, setting different CAV dedicated lanes under different CAV penetration rates, can increase traffic volume by 25.3% compared with the benchmark method. However, this paper is only an experimental analysis of a specific scenario. Next, we will try to mathematically model the general scene and express the experimental method with a mathematical model.

References

1. Smart Highway Project for 'Yancong' Highway (Beijing section) - China Highway Engineering Consultants Corporation (CHECC). http://techhighway.com.cn/index.php/article/1251/1480.html. Accessed 15 Jan 2020
2. Ioannou, P.A., Chien, C.C.: Autonomous intelligent cruise control. IEEE Trans. Veh. Technol. **42**(4), 657–672 (1993). https://doi.org/10.1109/25.260745
3. Marsden, G., McDonald, M., Brackstone, M.: Towards an understanding of adaptive cruise control. Transp. Res. Part C Emerg. Technol. **9**(1), 33–51 (2001). https://doi.org/10.1016/S0968-090X(00)00022-X
4. van Arem, B., van Driel, C.J.G., Visser, R.: The impact of cooperative adaptive cruise control on traffic-flow characteristics. IEEE Trans. Intell. Transport. Syst. **7**(4), 429–436 (2006). https://doi.org/10.1109/TITS.2006.884615
5. Kesting, A., Treiber, M., Schonhof, M., Helbing, D.: Adaptive cruise control design for active congestion avoidance. Transp. Res. C Emerg. Technol. (UK) **16**(6), 668–683 (2008). https://doi.org/10.1016/j.trc.2007.12.004
6. Shladover, S.E., Su, D., Lu, X.-Y.: Impacts of cooperative adaptive cruise control on freeway traffic flow. Transp. Res. Rec. **2324**(1), 63–70 (2012). https://doi.org/10.3141/2324-08
7. Talebpour, A., Mahmassani, H.S.: Influence of connected and autonomous vehicles on traffic flow stability and throughput. Transp. Res. Part C Emerg. Technol. **71**, 143–163 (2016). https://doi.org/10.1016/j.trc.2016.07.007
8. Chen, Z., He, F., Zhang, L., Yin, Y.: Optimal deployment of autonomous vehicle lanes with endogenous market penetration. Transp. Res. Part C Emerg. Technol. **72**, 143–156 (2016). https://doi.org/10.1016/j.trc.2016.09.013
9. Chen, D., Ahn, S., Chitturi, M., Noyce, D.A.: Towards vehicle automation: roadway capacity formulation for traffic mixed with regular and automated vehicles. Transp. Res. Part B Methodol. **100**, 196–221 (2017). https://doi.org/10.1016/j.trb.2017.01.017
10. Ghiasi, A., Hussain, O., Qian, Z.S., Li, X.: A mixed traffic capacity analysis and lane management model for connected automated vehicles: a Markov chain method. Transp. Res. Part B Methodol. **106**, 266–292 (2017). https://doi.org/10.1016/j.trb.2017.09.022

11. Talebpour, A., Mahmassani, H.S., Elfar, A.: Investigating the effects of reserved lanes for autonomous vehicles on congestion and travel time reliability. Transp. Res. Rec. **2622**(1), 1–12 (2017). https://doi.org/10.3141/2622-01
12. Kakimoto, Y., Iryo-Asano, M., Orhan, E., Nakamura, H.: A study on the impact of AV-HDV mixed traffic on flow dynamics of single-lane motorway. Transp. Res. Procedia **34**, 219–226 (2018). https://doi.org/10.1016/j.trpro.2018.11.035

Forecasting of Traffic Volume for Intelligent Transportation Systems via Support Vector Machine

Chuncheng Ma[✉]

CCCC First Highway Consultants Co. Ltd., Xi'an 710075, Shaanxi, China
496056424@qq.com

Abstract. Traffic volume forecasting is important to dynamically adjust traffic conditions for operations of intelligent transportation systems. To deal with this, this paper employed support vector machine (SVM) as the forecasting method. Then a case study was conducted for validating usefulness of this method, by using real data collected in Beijing, China. The measured traffic volumes and forecasting results were compared. Moreover, three evaluation indices were used to evaluate the forecasting accuracy. Results show the good accuracy of the method for forecasting traffic volumes in the case study. Based on the results obtained in this paper, it could provide reference for traffic volume forecasting for intelligent transportation systems.

Keywords: Intelligent transportation systems · Traffic volume forecasting · Support vector machine

1 Introduction

Traffic volume forecasting is useful to provide information for traffic control under intelligent transportation systems [1–3]. It means we use history data of traffic volume to forecast changes of volume in the near future. For short-term forecasting of traffic volume, the forecasting time could be 5 min or 15 min [4]. In this paper, we focus on 5 min of forecasting interval.

Many studies have been conducted for forecasting traffic volumes using various methods, including liner regress model [5], Kalman filtering [6], and neural network model [7], etc. Xie et al. proposed a forecasting method for short-term traffic volume forecasting based on Kalman filter [8]. Zhao et al. also focused on short-term traffic volume forecasting, which used a deep learning method [9]. Habtemichael and Cetin focused on identifying similar traffic patterns, and then they proposed new method for traffic volume forecasting [10]. Cai et al. also proposed a model for traffic volume forecasting, in which spatiotemporal correlative k-nearest neighbor model was presented [11].

Among these forecasting method, support vector machine (SVM) is a usual method and has been widely used for traffic flow forecasting [12–15]. According to good usefulness of SVM, we employ it as the forecasting method in this paper. Then real data collected in Beijing, China will be used for validation.

© Springer Nature Singapore Pte Ltd. 2020
J. Wang et al. (Eds.): GPC 2020 Workshops, CCIS 1311, pp. 67–72, 2020.
https://doi.org/10.1007/978-981-33-4532-4_6

The rest of this paper is as follows. The method of SVM will be firstly introduced in Sect. 2. Following this, a case study will be conducted to validate the method in Sect. 4. Finally, some conclusions can be obtained in Sect. 4.

2 Method of Support Vector Machine

The method of Support Vector Machine (SVM) was firstly proposed by Vapnik [16]. It has been widely used to forecast traffic flow in previous studies [12–15]. Then we also employ SVM as the method in this paper to conduct short-term traffic flow forecasting.

Generally speaking, we usually have a function to describe the forecasting of SVM at mathematics:

$$f(x) = \omega \cdot \varphi(x) + b_0 \tag{1}$$

When we use SVM to forecast something, we are solving the following optimization problem:

$$\min_{\substack{\omega \in R^n, \xi^{(*)} \in R^{2n}, b \in R \\ s.t.}} \begin{cases} \tau(\omega, \xi^{(*)}) = \dfrac{1}{2}||\omega||^2 + C\sum_{i=1}^{l}(\xi_i + \xi_i^*) \\ \omega \cdot \varphi(x_i) + b - y_i \le \varepsilon + \xi_i, \ i = 1, 2, \ldots, l \\ y_i - (\omega \cdot \varphi(x_i) + b) \le \varepsilon + \xi_i^*, \ i = 1, 2, \ldots, l \\ \xi^{(i)} \ge 0, \ i = 1, 2, \ldots, l \end{cases} \tag{2}$$

where $\xi^{(i)}$ is the slack variable and $\xi^{(i)} = (\xi_1, \xi_1^*, \ldots, \xi_i, \xi_i^*)^T$, C is the penalty parameter, ε is the channel width, $\varphi(x)$ is the map function.

To solve the above optimization problem, the Lagrange function is usually employed. Then the optimization problem would be transferred to dual problem, as follows:

$$\min_{\substack{\alpha^{(*)} \in R^{2l} \\ s.t.}} \begin{cases} \dfrac{1}{2}\sum_{i,j=1}^{l}(\alpha_i + \alpha_i^*)(\alpha_j - \alpha_j^*)K(x_i \cdot x_j) + \varepsilon\sum_{i=1}^{l}(\alpha_i + \alpha_i^*) + \sum_{i=1}^{l}y_i(\alpha_i - \alpha_i^*) \\ \sum_{i=1}^{l}(\alpha_i - \alpha_i^*) = 0 \\ 0 \le \alpha_i, \alpha_i^* \le C, i = 1, 2, \ldots, l \end{cases} \tag{3}$$

where $K(x_i \cdot x_j)$ is kernel function, which means $K(x_i \cdot x_j) = \varphi(x_i)^T\varphi(x_j)$, α_i and α_i^* are lagrange multipliers.

By calculating the above problem, we can obtain the following decision function:

$$f(x) = \sum_{i=1}^{l}(\overline{\alpha}_i^* - \overline{\alpha}_i)K(x_i \cdot x) + \overline{b} \tag{4}$$

where $\overline{\alpha}_i^*, \overline{\alpha}_i$, and $\overline{b}$ are solutions to dual problems.

When forecasting is focused based on SVM, we need substitute original data into independent variables of the decision function in Eq. (4). Then we can obtain the dependent variables of the decision function, which are actually the forecasting values that we need.

Moreover, in the applications of SVM, two more variables need to be selected. Based on previous studies [17–20], the Radial Basis Function (RBF) is considered as the kernel function in this paper. The Genetic Algorithm (GA) is used for parameters optimization method of SVM.

3   Case Study

3.1   Data and Evaluation Index

The data for forecasting and validation of SVM was obtained from real road in Beijing, China. The data contains traffic volumes in 15 days in May 2019. The forecasting interval is considered as 5 min. Then the traffic volumes are divided into several parts with 5 min for each. This means the data is sampled every 5 min. The total groups of these data are 540, among which the data of 14 days are used as training data and the data obtained in the last day is considered for validating. Then the traffic volumes at 5 min intervals are inputs of the SVM, while future forecasting values of traffic volumes also at 5 min intervals are outputs.

In order to smooth the data and improve calculation speed, the original data should normalize the data. The calculation formula is as follows:

$$y = \frac{(y_{max} - y_{min})(x - x_{min})}{x_{max} - x_{min}} + y_{min} \tag{5}$$

where x denotes the original data, and y denotes the normalized data, whose value is fixed as a range from -1 to 1.

It also needs some evaluation indices to validate the forecasting accuracy. We select three evaluation indices to deal with this question. The first one is MAE, the second index is MRE, and the third index is MSE. Their definitions are as follows:

$$\begin{cases} MAE = 1/N \sum_{i=1}^{N} |y_i - y'_i| \\ MRE = |y_i - y'_i|/y_i \times 100\% \\ MSE = 1/N \sum_{i=1}^{N} (y_i - y'_i)^2 \end{cases} \tag{6}$$

where y_i is measured value of traffic volume, y'_i is forecasting value of traffic volume, N is the total number of data.

3.2 Results

The forecasting calculations based on SVM are conducted in Matlab. According to simulation results, we compare measured traffic volume and forecasting results of traffic volume. Moreover, we also calculate the evaluations using Eq. (6). Then forecasting results of traffic volume are show in Fig. 1, compared with the measured volumes. The calculations of evaluation indices in Eq. (6) are shown in Table 1.

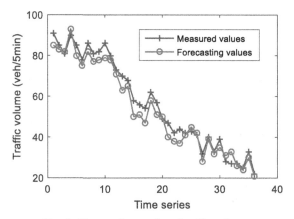

Fig. 1. Forecasting results of traffic volume.

Table 1. Calculations of evaluation indices.

MAE/veh	MRE/%	MSE
7.8143	0.2196	97.8109

Table 2. Results of comparison

Methods	MAE/veh	MRE/%	MSE
SVM	7.8143	0.2196	97.8109
Kalman filtering	9.6217	0.2852	121.3258

According to calculation results in Fig. 1 and Table 1, it is found that the errors between measured traffic volume and forecasting traffic volume are small. This means the SVM used in this paper has good accuracy for forecasting in our case study.

In order to compare performance of different methods, we compare forecasting accuracy between our method and the Kalman filtering method [6]. The results of comparison are shown in Table 2. According to results in Table 2, it can be found that SVM has better accuracy for forecasting traffic volume in the case of real data collected in Beijing, China.

4 Conclusion

This paper focuses on forecasting traffic volume using SVM method. In order to validate the usefulness of SVM method, the real data obtained in Beijing is used to conduct a case study. Results show the good accuracy for forecasting traffic volume. Specifically, the evaluation indices of *MAE*, *MRE*, and *MSE* are 7.8143, 0.2196, and 97.8109, respectively.

In addition to traffic volume, traffic flow conditions are usually evaluated by density. Then the forecasting for traffic flow density is needed to be study in the next step.

References

1. Kumar, S.V., Vanajakshi, L.: Short-term traffic flow prediction using seasonal ARIMA model with limited input data. Eur. Transp. Res. Rev. **7**(3), 1–9 (2015). https://doi.org/10.1007/s12 544-015-0170-8
2. Kumar, K., Parida, M., Katiyar, V.K.: Short term traffic flow prediction in heterogeneous condition using artificial neural network. Transport **30**(4), 397–405 (2015)
3. Kumar, S.V.: Traffic flow prediction using Kalman filtering technique. Procedia Eng. **187**, 582–587 (2017)
4. Bezuglov, A., Comert, G.: Short-term freeway traffic parameter prediction: application of Grey system theory models. Expert Syst. Appl. **62**, 284–292 (2016)
5. Apronti, D., Ksaibati, K., Gerow, K., Hepner, J.J.: Estimating traffic volume on Wyoming low volume roads using linear and logistic regression methods. J. Traffic Transp. Eng. (Engl. Ed.) **3**(6), 493–506 (2016)
6. Emami, A., Sarvi, M., Bagloee, S.A.: Using Kalman filter algorithm for short-term traffic flow prediction in a connected vehicle environment. J. Mod. Transp. **27**(3), 222–232 (2019). https://doi.org/10.1007/s40534-019-0193-2
7. Ma, X., Tao, Z., Wang, Y., Yu, H., Wang, Y.: Long short-term memory neural network for traffic speed prediction using remote microwave sensor data. Transp. Res. Part C Emerg. Technol. **54**, 187–197 (2015)
8. Xie, Y., Zhang, Y., Ye, Z.: Short-term traffic volume forecasting using Kalman filter with discrete wavelet decomposition. Comput.-Aided Civil Infrastruct. Eng. **22**(5), 326–334 (2007)
9. Zhao, Z., Chen, W., Wu, X., Chen, P.C., Liu, J.: LSTM network: a deep learning approach for short-term traffic forecast. IET Intel. Transp. Syst. **11**(2), 68–75 (2017)
10. Habtemichael, F.G., Cetin, M.: Short-term traffic flow rate forecasting based on identifying similar traffic patterns. Transp. Res. Part C Emerg. Technol. **66**, 61–78 (2016)
11. Cai, P., Wang, Y., Lu, G., Chen, P., Ding, C., Sun, J.: A spatiotemporal correlative k-nearest neighbor model for short-term traffic multistep forecasting. Transp. Res. Part C Emerg. Technol. **62**, 21–34 (2016)
12. Deshpande, M., Bajaj, P.: Performance improvement of traffic flow prediction model using combination of support vector machine and rough set. Int. J. Comput. Appl. **163**(2), 31–35 (2017)
13. Poonia, P., Jain, V.K., Kumar, A.: Short term traffic flow prediction methodologies: a review. Mody Univ. Int. J. Comput. Eng. Res. **2**(1), 37–39 (2018)
14. Feng, X., Ling, X., Zheng, H., Chen, Z., Xu, Y.: Adaptive multi-kernel SVM with spatial–temporal correlation for short-term traffic flow prediction. IEEE Trans. Intell. Transp. Syst. **20**(6), 2001–2013 (2018)
15. Tang, J., Chen, X., Hu, Z., Zong, F., Han, C., Li, L.: Traffic flow prediction based on combination of support vector machine and data denoising schemes. Physica A: Stat. Mech. Appl. **534**, 120642 (2019)

16. Pawar, D.S., Patil, G.R., Chandrasekharan, A., Upadhyaya, S.: Classification of gaps at uncontrolled intersections and midblock crossings using support vector machines. Transp. Res. Rec. **2515**(1), 26–33 (2015)
17. Kong, X., Xu, Z., Shen, G., Wang, J., Yang, Q., Zhang, B.: Urban traffic congestion estimation and prediction based on floating car trajectory data. Future Gener. Comput. Syst. **61**, 97–107 (2016)
18. Chen, D.: Research on traffic flow prediction in the big data environment based on the improved RBF neural network. IEEE Trans. Ind. Inform. **13**(4), 2000–2008 (2017)
19. Jung, H.C., Kim, J.S., Heo, H.: Prediction of building energy consumption using an improved real coded genetic algorithm based least squares support vector machine approach. Energy Build. **90**, 76–84 (2015)
20. Jiang, X., Zhang, L., Chen, X.M.: Short-term forecasting of high-speed rail demand: a hybrid approach combining ensemble empirical mode decomposition and gray support vector machine with real-world applications in China. Transp. Res. Part C: Emerg. Technol. **44**, 110–127 (2014)

Recovery Algorithm of Traffic Velocity Missing Data Based on Probe Vehicles

Jianzong Zhang, Manyi Qian, and Dan Tao[✉]

School of Electronic and Information Engineering, Beijing Jiaotong University, Beijing
100044, China
dtao@bjtu.edu.cn

Abstract. The popularity of GPS makes it possible to assess the condition of
urban roads based on vehicle data. In this paper, based on crowdsensing, we uses
probe vehicles data to evaluate urban traffic condition. To solve the problem of
missing traffic velocity data, this paper uses the taxies as probe vehicles to collect
GPS data, and proposes a Spatio-Temporal Correlation based on Compressed
Sensing algorithm (STC-CS) to recover missing data. Firstly, data preprocessing,
map matching, spatio-temporal division, and velocity calculation are performed
to obtain a traffic velocity matrix. Secondly, fully considering internal spatio-
temporal correlation among GPS data, we improve the sparse representation basis
of compressed sensing and model the problem of traffic velocity missing data
recovery as the problem of sparse vectors recovery. Based on a large-scale dataset,
we verify the effectiveness of the proposed algorithm. Experimental results show
that our STC-CS solution can achieve better recovery performance even if the
level of data missing is high.

Keywords: Crowdsensing · Data recovery · Compressed sensing ·
Spatio-temporal correlation

1 Introduction

Traditional traffic monitoring often relies on static sensors. However, it is not universal
because of high deployment and maintenance costs [1]. Crowdsensing takes the mobile
intelligent devices of users as basic perception units to realize data collection. Nowa-
days, GPS embedded in vehicles has been becoming increasingly popular. We can obtain
vehicle-related data to achieve road condition assessment by GPS, which has remark-
able advantages in low cost, convenient maintenance and flexible scalability [2]. It is a
common application to evaluate the traffic condition of city scale by using the data of the
probe vehicles [3]. Specifically, the probe vehicles are used to collect data periodically,
using the flow rate on a road segment in a certain period of time to characterize traffic
condition. Although the amount of traffic data involved is huge, traffic data for certain
road(s) at certain time segment(s) is still missing. Hence, how to recover traffic missing
data becomes a critical problem to be solved.

To effectively evaluate the traffic condition and obtain a complete map of the city
traffic, it is necessary to accurately recover the traffic missing data. In recent years,

© Springer Nature Singapore Pte Ltd. 2020
J. Wang et al. (Eds.): GPC 2020 Workshops, CCIS 1311, pp. 73–78, 2020.
https://doi.org/10.1007/978-981-33-4532-4_7

the collection and recovery of traffic velocity data have attracted widespread attention, and accumulated considerable research results. For example, *Wang et al.* [3] studied real-time road information acquisition base on crowdsensing and designed a reliability evaluation model to get traffic data. To achieve a wide range of road evaluation, *Zhu et al.* [4] employed the taxies as probe vehicles to collect data, then analyzed the structural characteristics of the traffic data in time and space and used low-rank matrix filling technology to infer the missing road information. However, this method was not ideal in high level of data missing. With the development of machine learning, more and more researchers try to learn data features to achieve data recovery [5, 6]. For example, *Zhang et al.* [6] adopted the convolutional neural network model to learn the taxi traffic flow model, and then predicted the traffic flow distribution matrix at the next moment. However, these rebuild processes were data sampling ones for "gridded" distribution nodes, which were different from the non-uniform sensing processes of probe vehicles.

Based on crowdsensing, we utilize the taxies as probe vehicles, and investigate a compressed sensing algorithm based on spatio-temporal correlation to recover traffic velocity missing data.

2   Traffic Velocity Missing Data Recovery Solution

In our work, probe vehicles which are used as traffic velocity monitors, is responsible for collecting a large number of traffic data. First of all, a traffic velocity matrix can be obtained through data preprocessing, map matching, spatio-temporal division, and velocity calculation. After spatial-temporal correlation analysis, the traffic velocity matrix will be restored by using compressed sensing algorithm. The framework of the recovery of traffic velocity missing data can be illustrated in Fig. 1.

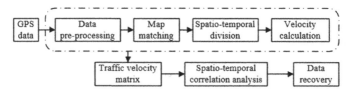

Fig. 1. Framework of the recovery of traffic velocity missing data.

2.1   Traffic Velocity Matrix Acquisition

Based on the crowdsensing, this paper uses the data of the probe vehicles which are taxies to evaluate the road condition. The data source includes about 250,000 pieces of data collected by 1,000 taxies in Dongguan city in 10 days [7], covering the range of longitude 23.0°–23.07° E and latitude 113.7°–113.84° N, which are all over the urban area of Dongguan. The GPS data includes information such as carID, time, latitude, longitude, speed and direction. First, some abnormal data will be eliminated, such as invalid data and noisy data. Second, deviation points can be corrected by using Kalman filtering for subsequent velocity calculation. Third, road nodes can serve as demarcation points in spatio-temporal division to divide multiple road segments and time interval is set as 5 min. Finally, the traffic velocity of each road segment at different time segments can be calculated to construct a 2-dimensional traffic velocity matrix S. Table 1 shows an example of a traffic velocity matrix, where "?" denotes missing data.

Table 1. Example of a traffic velocity matrix.

V(km/h)		Time segment ID				
		Time_1	Time_2	Time_3	Time_4	......
Road segment ID	road_1	?	15	?	57	......
	road_2	?	?	?	32	......
	road_3	?	?	?	?	......
	road_4	16	?	?	18	......
	......	......	......	......	......	......

2.2 Spatio-Temporal Correlation Analysis

To reveal spatio-temporal correlation among traffic velocity data, Pearson correlation coefficient is used to characterize the similarity of two 2D vectors, which can be calculated as follows:

$$R = \frac{cov(x, y)}{\sigma_x \sigma_y} = \frac{\Sigma_{i=1}^{n}(x_i - \bar{x})(y_i - \bar{y})}{\sqrt{\Sigma_{i=1}^{n}(x_i - \bar{x})^2 \Sigma_{i=1}^{n}(y_i - \bar{y})^2}} \tag{1}$$

where $cov(x,y)$ is the covariance of 2D vectors x, y, and σ_x, σ_y, $\bar{x}$, $\bar{y}$ are variances and averages of x and y, respectively.

Here, 7 adjacent time segments for a same road segment and 7 adjacent road segments for a same time segment are selected to calculate their corresponding correlation coefficients. In Fig. 2 and Fig. 3, the statistical results show that the closer two adjacent time (road) segments are, the stronger their spatio (temporal) correlation will become. Specifically, R of the most of adjacent 3 road (time) segments is larger than 0.8.

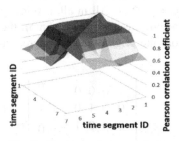

Fig. 2. Time correlation statistics.

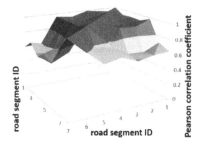

Fig. 3. Space correlation statistics.

2.3 Data Recovery

There exists strong spatio-temporal correlation among traffic data, which can be utilized to improve the sparse representation basis of compressed sensing. We model the recovery problem of traffic velocity missing data as sparse vectors recovery one.

Traffic velocity usually has time-domain smoothness, that is, only a few velocity values will change greatly in two adjacent time segments. Therefore, a time sparse basis matrix T can be described as formula (2).

$$T = \begin{bmatrix} 1 & -1 & 0 & \cdots & 0 \\ 0 & 1 & -1 & \ddots & \vdots \\ 0 & 0 & 1 & \ddots & 0 \\ \vdots & \vdots & \ddots & \ddots & \vdots \\ 0 & 0 & \cdots & 0 & 1 \end{bmatrix} \tag{2}$$

Then, the projection of the ith row S_i of velocity matrix S under matrix T is $\gamma_t = T S_i$. Let $\varphi_t = T^{-1}$, so S_i can be expressed sparsely as $S_i = \varphi_t \gamma_t$.

In velocity matrix S, there is a certain topology which reveals spatial correlation among road segments. A spatial sparse matrix H can be defined as formula (3):

$$H = h((x,y))_{n*n} = \begin{cases} 1, x \text{ is adjacent to } y \\ 0, other \end{cases} \tag{3}$$

In this way, a sparse basis of traffic velocity matrix φ can be obtained by Kronecker product operation, that is, $\varphi = \varphi_t \otimes H$. All in all, a velocity matrix can be expressed sparsely as $S_i = \varphi\alpha$. Because of the missing data in S_i, the known data can be used as measured values to restore the original matrix. Here, an observation matrix ψ_i is designed for S_i as follows:

$$\psi_i = \begin{bmatrix} 1 & 0 & 0 & 0 & \cdots & 0 \\ 0 & 0 & 1 & 0 & \ddots & \vdots \\ 0 & 0 & 0 & 1 & \ddots & 0 \\ \vdots & \vdots & \vdots & \vdots & \ddots & \vdots \\ 0 & 0 & 0 & 0 & 0 & 0 \end{bmatrix} \tag{4}$$

where if (m, n) in matrix ψ_i values 1, it means that the mth observation can be obtained in the nth time segment. So, we can get an observation matrix ψ_k for the complete traffic velocity matrix S:

$$\psi_k = \begin{bmatrix} \psi_1 & 0 & \cdots & 0 \\ 0 & \psi_2 & \ddots & \vdots \\ \vdots & \vdots & \ddots & \vdots \\ 0 & \cdots & 0 & \psi_n \end{bmatrix} \tag{5}$$

Let y represent the observation value of S_i. An observation vector of S_i can be expressed as $y = \psi \varphi \alpha$. Knowing y, ψ, φ, we can get α by solving a convex optimization problem. In this way, we can recover traffic velocity missing data.

3 Experimental Simulation

In this section, some simulations are performed to testify the performance of our STC-CS algorithm. To quantify the accuracy of data recovery, three popular performance evaluation criteria are applied, they are MAE, RMSE and MAPE. In different levels of data missing, we compare the performance of our STC-CS algorithm with those of Statistical Interpolation (SI), K-Nearest Neighbor (KNN) and grey residual GM(1,N) [8] model.

Table 2. Comparison on different data recovery algorithms when the level of data missing is 50%.

ALGORITHM	MAE	RMSE	MPAE
SI	12.32	16.21	0.17
KNN	6.61	9.88	0.09
GM(1,N)	3.56	3.01	0.03
STC-CS	3.33	3.88	0.03

Table 3. Comparison on different data recovery algorithms when the level of data missing is 80%.

ALGORITHM	MAE	RMSE	MPAE
SI	22.31	27.21	0.21
KNN	11.21	9.88	0.13
GM(1,N)	4.34	5.41	0.12
STC-CS	3.87	5.12	0.09

Here, we select two different levels of data missing, they are 50% and 80%, respectively. The experimental results are given in Table 2 and Table 3. We can conclude that the greater the level of data missing is, the worse the recovery performance gets. SI algorithm and KNN algorithm have lower accuracy in view of insufficient consideration of spatio-temporal correlation. When the level of data missing is 50%, MPAEs of GM(1,N) and our STC-CS algorithm are equivalent. However, our STC-CS algorithm is better than GM(1,N) on MAE and RMSE. When the level of data missing is 80%, STC-CS algorithm performs better than other three algorithms. The recovered data is closer to the actual traffic velocity data.

4   Conclusion

In this paper, we utilize the probe vehicles technology to evaluate the traffic condition based on crowdsensing. To solve the recovery problem of traffic velocity missing data, this paper presents a compressed sensing algorithm based on spatio-temporal correlation. Experimental results testify the performance of our solution, which can provide an efficient way for road condition assessment.

Acknowledgment. This work was partly supported by the National Natural Science Foundation of China under Grant No.61872027.

References

1. Hu, J., Tao, D.: Theories and methods of quality measure and assurance for mobile crowd sensing. J. Chin. Comput. Syst. **40**(5), 918–923 (2019)
2. Tong, C.F., Xu, Y., Li, J., et al.: Internet-based urban bus travelling data acquisition and missing data recovery. In: International Conference on Mobile Ad-hoc & Sensor Networks, pp. 343–347. IEEE (2017)
3. Wang, X., Zhang, J., Tian, X.: Crowdsensing-based consensus incident report for road traffic acquisition. IEEE Trans. Intell. Transp. Syst. **19**(18), 1–12 (2017)
4. Zhu, Y., Li, Z., Zhu, H., et al.: A compressive sensing approach to urban traffic estimation with probe vehicles. IEEE Trans. Mob. Comput. **12**(11), 2289–2302 (2013)
5. Zhang, J., Zheng, Y., Qi, D.: Deep spatio-temporal residual networks for citywide crowd flows prediction. In: Proceedings of the Thirty-First Conference on Artificial Intelligence, February 4–9, 2017. San Francisco, California, USA, pp. 1655-1661 (2017)
6. Zhang, C., Ouyang, X., Patras, P.: ZipNet-GAN: inferring fine-grained mobile traffic patterns via a generative adversarial neural network. In: Proceedings of the 13th International Conference on emerging Networking Experiments and Technologies, CoNEXT December 12–15, 2017. Incheon, Republic of Korea, pp. 363-375 (2017)
7. OpenData2[EB/OL]. http://www.openits.cn/openData2/604.jhtml. Accessed 1 May 2019
8. Guo, M., Lan, J., Li, J., et al.: Traffic flow data recovery algorithm based on grey residual GM(1, N) model. Transp. Syst. Eng. Inform. Technol. **01**, 46–51 (2012)

The Influence of Text Length on Text Classification Model

Tingyue Liu$^{(\boxtimes)}$, Yunji Liang, and Zhiwen Yu

School of Computer Science, Northwestern Polytechnical University, Xi'an 710129, China
tingyueliu@outlook.com

Abstract. In this paper, we detect the mental health status of the posters based on social media. Due to the wide range of textual data length in social media, we prove that the length of text input has an effect on the main deep learning architectures such as Convolutional Neural Network (CNN) and Recurrent Neural Network (RNN) used in text classification. We argue through three distinct indicators in the English standard dataset and Reddit mental illness dataset, including accuracy, model parameter complexity and time complexity, and set the maximum length of text input on the text classification models by changing the proportion of train-ing/test dataset. As text grows, the accuracy of text classification algorithms also tends to increase, as does the time complexity and model parameter complexity overhead. The shorter maximum length of text results in lower accuracy, while the longer maximum text length leads to higher training costs of algorithms. It allows us to find that the common text classification algorithm models have shown signif-icant influence on the standard English dataset and Reddit mental illness dataset. The length of text or a string, especially for controlling the maximum length of text input on the models separately, puts a strict limit on the text classification algorithm.

Keywords: Mental illness · Text length · Text classification · Accuracy

1 Introduction

With the rapid development of society and the acceleration of the pace of life, the mental health problem has become one of the important reasons that endanger human health. The number of people suffering from mental illness is growing all over the world. According to the statistics of the World Health Organization (WHO), there are about 340 million individuals with depression worldwide by 2019. Depression has become a common mental illness, but it is not taken seriously by the majority of the population. An international study in 2018 [1] has showed that graduate students are six times more likely to exhibit depression symptoms than the general population, and respondents with moderate to severe depression or anxiety account for 40% of the total. In 2020, the COVID-19 coronavirus epidemic, as a source of acute stress, has greatly affected the physical and mental health of the social masses. Compared with healthy folks, patients with mental illness might suffer more serious consequences, such as agitation, disease

© Springer Nature Singapore Pte Ltd. 2020
J. Wang et al. (Eds.): GPC 2020 Workshops, CCIS 1311, pp. 79–90, 2020.
https://doi.org/10.1007/978-981-33-4532-4_8

recurrence and increased risk of suicide. The impact of the epidemic on mentally ill needs to be widely paid attention by the industry and the society [2].

Mental illnesses refer to "a wide range of mental health conditions that affect mood, thinking, behavior and relationship with others" and pose devastating threats to the personal wellbeing [3]. The traditional screening and assessment of mental illness mostly use questionnaires or professional scales to match the user's clinical manifestations with the typical symptoms described in the diagnostic manual. However, this kind of evaluation method has quite a few problems, such as lower timeliness, higher cost, lower visiting rate and higher misdiagnosis rate. As the development of intelligent perception technology and social media platforms, it is possible to continuously detect and track the mental state of the users. The journal of the American Medical Association (JAMA) has put forward the concept of "Digital Phenotyping", and it is proposed to perceive, track and predict mental illness by analyzing the "Digital footprint" formed by users in the interaction with electronic devices [4]. Especially, with the widespread of smart phones and wearable devices, behavioral-based detection methods are to use electronic devices to continuously evaluate and quantify human behaviors. A multitude of studies demonstrate that patients with depression have difficulties in emotional cognition and expression. Consequently, it is a crucial approach to detect individual emotional abnormalities based on facial expressions and voice characteristics. Electronic medical record-based detection methods used to analyze data obtained from patient charts and the electronic medical record. Whereas, all the above three detection methods have some significant limitations. The sensor data is sparse, and it is too difficult to extract the sound characteristics in the case of mixed speech. The limitations of facial expression and electronic medical record data are mainly reflected in the incompleteness and discontinuity. In addition, the narrative written by the clinician does not directly record the patient's own experience, but only a professional description at the point of care.

In view of the limitations of the above three methods, a detection method based on social media is proposed. Social media data is rich and constant, which represents the continuous status of users. Social media platforms have become a major source of daily communication today, and linking behavior patterns of social media to stress, anxiety, depression, suicide and other mental illness may offer a new opportunity to reduce undiagnosed mental illness. Social media-based detection method is to study the relationship between linguistic features and mental health states, and to find the correlation between grammatical features, emotional features, sentence complexity, language consistency and mental illness. A paper published in the Proceedings of the National Academy of Sciences (PNAS) built a prediction model based on the linguistic characteristics, including text content, post length, post frequency, and post time pattern on Facebook, which could be effective for depression detection [5]. G. Gkotsis et al. [6] adopted a convolutional neural network (CNN) method based on Reddit textual data to classify posts related to mental health.

Based on social media (Twitter, Facebook, Reddit, etc.), textual data is classified into two categories (whether mental illness or not) and multiple categories (mental illness category). It has become an important research direction to mine the information we care about from these massive textual data. Text mining is a process of automatically mining potentially new information from textual data. It uses techniques from information retrieval, information extraction as well as natural language processing (NLP) and connects them with the algorithms and methods of KDD, data mining, machine learning and statistics [7]. Due to the high-dimensional, sparse, and unstructured characteristics of textual data, compared with traditional data mining, text mining is unique in that the text is semi-structured or unstructured, has no definite form and lacks machine-understandable semantics. The objects of data mining are mainly structured data in the database, and use relational tables and other storage structures to discover knowledge. As an application-driven method, text mining has been widely used in information retrieval, business intelligence, etc., such as sentiment classification, spam filtering, and search engines.

As a key text mining task, text classification is one of the most used techniques in the field of text information processing. It is also one of the most common and typical problems in natural language processing. The task of text classification is to automatically determine the text-related categories based on the content of the text under a given classification system. Traditional text classification method uses the characteristics of manual design, which can be divided into two steps: feature engineering and classifier. Among them, the text feature engineering is divided into three parts: text preprocessing, feature extraction and text representation. The purpose is to convert the text into a computer-understandable format, so that it has a strong feature expression ability, such as bag-of-words [8]. Classifiers are machine learning methods, such as Naive Bayes classification algorithm [9], SVM [10], decision tree [11]. However, the main problem of the traditional method is text representation, whose feature expression ability is very weak. It requires manual feature engineering and costs a lot.

So far, deep learning algorithms, especially Convolutional Neural Network (CNN) and Recurrent Neural Network (RNN) [12, 13] have shown excellent effects on text classification. Different from traditional machine learning methods, the most important part of deep learning method to solve text classification problem is text representation. It means that each word is represented as word embedding, such as word2vec [14] and GloVe [15]. Text representation changes the textual data from high-latitude and high-sparse features to continuous dense vector. CNN, RNN and other deep learning network structures are used to automatically acquire the feature expression capability, which avoids the tedious feature extraction process. Based on the word embedding technology, the multi-layer neural network with Sigmoid function is used to extract the high dimensional features.

However, the length of the text puts a great restriction on the classification model because the length of social media textual data varies. The existing text classification methods has the following problems: (1) the time series model (such as LSTM, GRU, etc.) can be used for short text containing dozens of words (such as microblogging data and Tweet data). Instead, as the text grows, the training efficiency of time series model is too low to be applied well in order to tackle long document. The reason is that RNN cannot be parallelized well and the time of operation cost will be longer. (2) the efficient and commonly used model for long text classification is Convolutional Neural Network (CNN), which is due to the high parallelization of this model. Whereas, the problem with CNN is that the input of the convolutional layer is a fixed filter size, which means that it cannot be modeled against a sequence with a longer convolutional filter size.

Therefore, we propose that the length of text or a string puts a strict limit on the text classification algorithm models. By the experimental method, it proves that the input length of text has a significant impact on the standard text classification algorithm in English standard dataset and Reddit mental illness dataset.

2 Related Works

Text classification is a very classic problem in the field of natural language processing (NLP). Its related research can be traced back to the 1950s, when it was classified by patterns [16]. The advantage of this method is that it can solve the top problem in a short time, but it takes a lot of time and effort, and the coverage and accuracy are very limited.

Later, with the development of statistical learning methods, especially the increase in the number of online textual data on the Internet and the rise of machine learning methods [17], a set of machine learning methods to solve text classification problems have gradually been formed. The steps at this stage are artificial feature engineering and classification models. Artificial feature engineering is divided into three parts: text preprocessing, feature extraction, and text representation. Its purpose is to convert the textual data into a computer-understandable format, and has a strong feature expression ability. Text preprocessing is the process of extracting keywords from text to represent text, which mainly includes two stages: text segmentation and stop word removal. Especially, stop words are some high-frequency pronoun and con-junctions in the text, which are meaningless to the text classification, so we usually maintain a stop word list. Feature extraction is to rank the original vocabulary items independently according to a certain evaluation index, select some feature items with the highest score, and filter out the remaining feature items. Commonly used evaluations include term frequency-inverse document frequency (TF-IDF), information gain, and χ^2 statistics [18]. In traditional text representation, there are text representation methods based on semantics, such as LDA topic model [19]. In terms of classifiers, most machine learning methods have used in the field of text classification, such as Naive Bayes classification algorithm [9], SVM [10], decision tree [11]. The traditional text classification method has weak feature expression ability, and requires manual feature engineering, which is very costly. Deep learning algorithm to solve the text classification problem is to use CNN/RNN and other neural network structures to automatically obtain feature expression capabilities, eliminating complex artificial feature engineering.

Recurrent Neural Network (RNN) is an algorithm which is to solve the problem of modeling variable length input sequence. It passes the sequence information generated in each step to the next step. For shorter text with dozens of words, the time series model has been generally used on text classification. In 2015, an emotion classification model was proposed to use GRU to model text classification [13]. Tai et al. [20] proposed the tree structure LSTM (a variant of RNN) to improve semantic representation. Liu et al. [21] used three different sharing information mechanisms based on RNN were proposed for text multi-classification task to model specific text. The emergence of RNN is to solve the problem of variable length sequence information modeling. However, as the text gets longer, the operation time cost will be very larger because RNN cannot parallelize well. And the training efficiency of models like time series model is lower, which cannot be applied well.

Convolutional Neural Network (CNN) has been widely used on the long text classification. The model of using CNN on text classification was firstly presented by Kim [12]. Lai et al. [22] proposed a classification method of recurrent convolutional neural network without artificial features, called RCNN. It uses Bi-RNN to capture the characterization, and then apply the convolution operation to input to obtain the probability variable of the label. Yang et al. [23] showed a hierarchical attention mechanism network for document classification, referred to as HAN. Johnson et al. [24] used a deep Convolutional Neural Network model of word level named DPCNN, which could capture the global representation of the text. Whereas the problem of CNN is mentioned above, the length of input sequence is fixed resulted from filter size of convolution layer. Even if the features of different ranges are obtained through multiple convolution layers, it is necessary to pay the cost of increasing the depth of the neural network.

In recent years, from the perspective of convolutional layer, the convolution kernel is changed to optimize. Aiming at the problem that traditional convolutional neural networks use static windows for convolution, Wang et al. [25] proposed a CNN model with attention mechanism of multi-scale features. By establishing a cross-layer connection between the low-level features and high-level features, rich multi-scale features are obtained, and the attention model can adaptively select the appropriate scale features to be applicable to various text classification problems. Du et al. [26] used a hierarchical gated convolutional network with multiple attention mechanisms to reduce the computational cost. It has a word-level and sentence-level text hierarchy, which overcomes the shortcomings of CNN's fixed input size. Choi et al. [27] proposed an adaptive convolution method for text classification. Adaptive convolution is based on input and uses adaptively generated convolution kernels.

Consequently, in terms of text classification, Recurrent Neural Network is not suitable for long text classification. Adaptive convolution kernels are of great significance in convolutional neural networks. Motivated by this, we try to show whether the length of text has any effect on the text classification algorithm models.

3   Proposed Method

3.1   Task Definition and Primarily Input

Text classification task is to automatically classify text sets according to a certain classification system or standard. The problem of text classification is de-fined as follows. Given a set of text document $D = \{D1, D2, ..., Dn\}$, and each document is tagged with a label. Each tag is labeled from a set of x different labels $\{L1, L2, ..., Lx\}$. According to a set of training documents that have been annotated, the relationship model between document characteristics and document categories is found, and then the unclassified documents are judged according to the relationship model obtained from this learning. The primary input of our method is textual dataset and a fixed set of classes. Our task of text classification is to identify a predicted class.

3.2   Method Overview

In our work, we need to determine the effect of the length of text input on the text classification algorithm model. First of all, the selected dataset is sorted in ascending order by text length. Then, taking the ratio of the training-set to the test-set as 1:1 as an example, the dataset with the first 1/2 as the training-set and the dataset with the second 1/2 as the test-set. And the number of words in the critical documents of the training-set and test-set is called maxlen. Let the ratio of the training set to the test set increase gradually, and find each maxlen value in turn. Figure 1 shows overall workflow of our approach. In addition to the above method, we use short-text classification and long-text classification as described in the next section.

Fig. 1. Overall workflow of our approach

3.3   Short-Text Classification and Long-Text Classification

For text classification, how to extract features is a main and important problem. The biggest advantage of deep learning method on text classification is that it avoids the tedious feature extraction process and uses continuous vectors for embedding presentation. However, the length of the text puts a big limit on the classification model. In this section, we will explain the background knowledge of short-text classification and long-text classification and how to determine the impact of text input length on the text classification model.

Short-Text Classification: The short text usually refers to the text form with a short length of no more than 160 characters, such as microblog, chat, news topic, opinion comment, literature abstract, etc. The purpose of the short-text classification task is to automatically process the short text input by the user and get the correct output category. The features of the short text data are sparsity and real-time. Sparsity is reflected in the short length of the short text, which usually contains only a few to a dozen words with practical significance, so it is difficult to extract effective feature words. Real-time is that its update speed is fast and easy to spread. And due to the timely update and rapid dissemination of short text, the Internet has accumulated a large number of short textual data, which requires the short text processing and calculation must have a very high speed. A time series model (LSTM, etc.) is usually used for short-text classification, but as the text grows longer, the Recurrent Neural Network (RNN) model cannot be parallelized well.

Long-Text Classification: Long text usually exist in news text, document text, blog text, etc., and contain dozens or even hundreds of sentences. Consistent with the final purpose of the short text classification task, it is to automatically process long text and obtain the correct output category. However, it contains a lot of information, which is irrelevant to the subject and affects the classification effect and performance. For longer textual data, CNN model is usually used, but the input size is fixed in convolution, and the establishment of long sequence model will generate a large number of parameters.

4 Experiments

4.1 Lab Environment

The algorithm models used in this paper are all implemented using Python programming, and the neural network is partially built using open source TensorFlow module. The main parameters of the model training and computing environment on the English standard dataset and Reddit mental illness dataset is the GPU whose memory is 16 GB.

4.2 Dataset

The English standard dataset provided by Andrew et al., 2011 [28] and Reddit mental illness dataset through crawling the website were tested on, the brief description is as follows:

IMDB: IMDB English dataset is 50,000 comments from the online movie database, which is used for sentiment analysis. The sentiment of the comment is binary, which means that the IMDB rating < 5 results in a sentiment score of 0, while the sentiment score of rating $> = 7$ is 1. No movie has more than 30 reviews. There are 25,000 used for training and 25,000 used for testing in the original dataset. With positive and negative comments accounting for 50% of each section.

Reddit: Based on review data from Reddit on the mental health section from 2013 to 2017, it contains 31918 comment documents. We selected four mental illness classification categories: Attention Deficit Hyperactivity Disorder (ADHD), anxiety, depression and Post-Traumatic Stress Disorder (PTSD). There are 15959 in the dataset for training and 15959 for testing.

The English standard dataset IMDB and Reddit mental illness dataset are selected, and the text length distribution range is very wide. In order to improve the data analysis of the text length of the datasets, we use three statistical indicators to describe the text length of the two datasets in finer-grained description. The average reflects the central tendency. The standard deviation reflects the degree of dispersion of the dataset. And the quartiles describe the distribution of the dataset as a whole (Table 1).

Table 1. Statistics of our datasets

Dataset	Number of categories	Dataset size (number of texts)	Text length range (number of words)	Average text length (number of words)	Standard deviation of text length (number of words)	Quartile of text length (number of words)
IMDB	2	50000	6–2470	215	2255	115, 160, 262
Reddit	4	31918	1–2809	154.024	148.9388	60, 114,119

4.3 Settings

First of all, for the English standard dataset IMDB and Reddit mental illness dataset, before the training stage, the corpus of the training-set and the test-set needs to be preprocessed and textually represented. The text is represented as word embedding and the useless information needs to be removed to reduce the complexity and computational burden of subsequent steps. In the phase of removing stop words, the purpose is to make the auxiliary words in the language drop some very poor expressive ability from the original text. For English stop words, we maintain the corresponding stop word list. After the pre-steps, the training-set text and the test-set text are expressed as word embedding.

To determine the effect of text input length on the text classification algorithm model, we arranged the selected dataset in ascending order of text length. The shorter text data is the training-set, and the longer text is the test-set. The ratio of training-set to test-set is always 1: 1 to ensure that the size of the test-set is the same every time. Change the maximum length of the text input, called maxlen. It is the length of the phrase used for padding, and if the value is shorter, it is used to crop the text. The method to determine the maxlen value is to adjust the ratio of the training-set and the test-set, in order from 1, 1/2,…, 1/6 to the critical value of the training-set and the test-set as the maxlen value of each time. In the IMDB dataset, maxlen (the number of words) is 150, 225, 285, 325, 360, and 400. And in the Reddit dataset, maxlen (the number of words) is 114, 164, 199, 227, 251, and 270, respectively.

CNN [12], LSTM [21], Bi-LSTM [29] and RCNN [22] models have been applied in the training-set and test-set, and the value of maxlen is changed in turn. The algorithm accuracy (P), model parameter complexity and time complexity were used for evaluation. The calculation method is shown in formula (1).

$$P = \frac{X}{X + Y} \tag{1}$$

Among them, X represents the number of texts correctly classified into this category, Y represents the number of texts classified into this category by mistake.

4.4   Results

The results of the text classification experiment in the IMDB dataset are shown in Figs. 2, 3, and 4. Figure 2 shows the algorithm accuracy. Figure 3 shows the model parameter complexity. Figure 4 shows the time complexity. The results of the text classification experiment in the Reddit mental illness dataset are shown in Figs. 5, 6, and 7. Figure 5 shows the algorithm accuracy. Figure 6 shows the model parameter complexity. Figure 7 shows the time complexity.

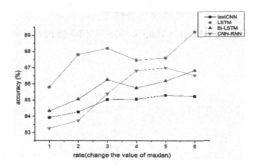

Fig. 2. The algorithm accuracy of IMDB dataset

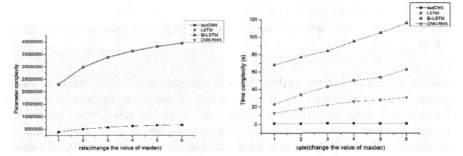

Fig. 3. The parameter complexity of IMDB dataset   **Fig. 4.** The time complexity of IMDB dataset

As the maximum length of text input grows on the IMDB and Reddit mental illness dataset, the accuracy of some general algorithms (CNN, LSTM, Bi-LSTM and RCNN) for text classification will increase, as will the model parameter complexity and time complexity. Conversely, the shorter the maximum text length, the lower the accuracy.

5   Discussion

In this paper, we leverage social media textual data to detect and classify the mental health status of users. Based on the varying length of textual data on social media, we prove that the length of text input makes an influence on the common deep learning architectures to solve text classification problem. By sorting the datasets, we change the maximum length of the text input, and demonstrate it on the English standard dataset and Reddit

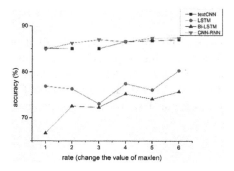

Fig. 5. The algorithm accuracy of Reddit dataset

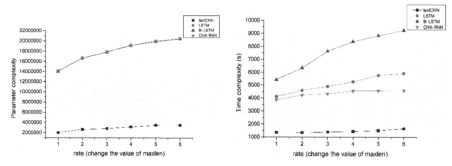

Fig. 6. The parameter complexity of Reddit dataset

Fig. 7. The time complexity of Reddit dataset

mental illness dataset in terms of three different indicators of accuracy, model parameter complexity and time complexity. It is found that the length of text input will have a certain impact on the text classification algorithm model by conducting experimental research. The text will become longer, the training cost will increase, and the accuracy will also rise. The result demonstrates that our proposed method can verify the validity of this hypothesis.

References

1. Evans, T.M., Bira, L., Gastelum, J.B., et al.: Evidence for a mental health crisis in graduate education. Nat. Biotechnol. **36**(3), 282–284 (2018)
2. Wang, Q., Li, X.B.: Effects of acute stress on patients with mental illness. Chin. J. Psychiatry **53**(00), E006–E006 (2020). (in Chinese)
3. Liang, Y., Zheng, X., Zeng, D.D.: A survey on big data-driven digital phenotyping of mental health. Inf. Fusion **52**, 290–307 (2019)
4. Insel, T.R.: Digital phenotyping: technology for a new science of behavior. JAMA **318**(13), 1215–1216 (2017)
5. Eichstaedt, J.C., et al.: Facebook language predicts depression in medical records. PNAS **115**(44), 11203–11208 (2018)

6. Gkotsis, G., et al.: Characterisation of mental health conditions in social media using Informed Deep Learning. Sci. Rep. **7**, 46813 (2017)
7. Hotho, A., Nürnberger, A., Paaß, G.: A brief survey of text mining. In: LDV Forum, vol. 20, no. 1, pp. 19–62 (2005)
8. McCallum, A.: Bow: A toolkit for statistical language modeling, text retrieval, classification and clustering (1996). http://www.cs.cmu.edu/~mccallum/bow
9. McCallum, A., Nigam, K.: A comparison of event models for Naive Bayes text classification. In: AAAI 1998 Workshop on Learning for Text Categorization, vol. 752, no. 1, pp. 41–48 (1998)
10. Joachims, T.: A statistical learning learning model of text classification for support vector machines. In: Proceedings of the 24th Annual International ACM SIGIR Conference on Research and Development in Information Retrieval, pp. 128–136 (2001)
11. Johnson, D.E., Oles, F.J., Zhang, T., et al.: A decision-tree-based symbolic rule induction system for text categorization. IBM Syst. J. **41**(3), 428–437 (2002)
12. Kim, Y.: Convolutional neural networks for sentence classification. arXiv preprint arXiv: 1408.5882 (2014)
13. Tang, D., Qin, B., Liu, T.: Document modeling with gated recurrent neural network for sentiment classification. In: Proceedings of the 2015 Conference on Empirical Methods in Natural Language Processing, pp. 1422–1432 (2015)
14. Mikolov, T., Chen, K., Corrado, G., et al.: Efficient estimation of word representations in vector space. arXiv preprint arXiv:1301.3781 (2013)
15. Pennington, J., Socher, R., Manning, C.D.: GloVe: global vectors for word representation. In: Proceedings of the 2014 Conference on Empirical Methods in Natural Language Processing (EMNLP), pp. 1532–1543 (2014)
16. Sasaki, M., Kita, K.: Rule-based text categorization using hierarchical categories. In: SMC 1998 Conference Proceedings, 1998 IEEE International Conference on Systems, Man, and Cybernetics (Cat. No. 98CH36218), vol. 3, pp. 2827–2830. IEEE (1998)
17. Ikonomakis, M., Kotsiantis, S., Tampakas, V.: Text classification using machine learning techniques. WSEAS Trans. Comput. **4**(8), 966–974 (2005)
18. Aggarwal, C.C., Zhai, C.: A survey of text classification algorithms. In: Aggarwal, C., Zhai, C. (eds.) Mining Text Data, pp. 163–222. Springer, Boston (2012). https://doi.org/10.1007/978-1-4614-3223-4_6
19. Blei, D.M., Ng, A.Y., Jordan, M.I.: Latent Dirichlet allocation. J. Mach. Learn. Res. **3**, 993–1022 (2003)
20. Tai, K.S., Socher, R., Manning, C.D.: Improved semantic representations from tree-structured long short-term memory networks. arXiv preprint arXiv:1503.00075 (2015)
21. Liu, P., Qiu, X., Huang, X.: Recurrent neural network for text classification with multi-task learning. arXiv preprint arXiv:1605.05101 (2016)
22. Lai, S., Xu, L., Liu, K., et al.: Recurrent convolutional neural networks for text classification. In: Twenty-Ninth AAAI Conference on Artificial Intelligence (2015)
23. Yang, Z., Yang, D., Dyer, C., et al.: Hierarchical attention networks for document classification. In: Proceedings of the 2016 Conference of the North American Chapter of the Association for Computational Linguistics: Human Language Technologies, pp. 1480–1489 (2016)
24. Johnson, R., Zhang, T.: Deep pyramid convolutional neural networks for text categorization. In: Proceedings of the 55th Annual Meeting of the Association for Computational Linguistics (Volume 1: Long Papers), pp. 562–570 (2017)
25. Wang, S., Huang, M., Deng, Z.: Densely connected CNN with multi-scale feature attention for text classification. In: IJCAI, pp. 4468–4474 (2018)
26. Du, H., Qian, J.: Hierarchical gated convolutional networks with multi-head attention for text classification. In: 2018 5th International Conference on Systems and Informatics (ICSAI), pp. 1170–1175. IEEE (2018)

27. Choi, B.J., Park, J.H., Lee, S.K.: Adaptive convolution for text classification. In: Proceedings of the 2019 Conference of the North American Chapter of the Association for Computational Linguistics: Human Language Technologies, Volume 1 (Long and Short Papers), pp. 2475–2485 (2019)
28. Maas, A.L., Daly, R.E., Pham, P.T., et al.: Learning word vectors for sentiment analysis. In: Proceedings of the 49th Annual Meeting of the Association for Computational Linguistics: Human Language Technologies, vol. 1, pp. 142–150. Association for Computational Linguistics (2011)
29. Xu, G., Meng, Y., Qiu, X., et al.: Sentiment analysis of comment texts based on BiLSTM. IEEE Access **7**, 51522–51532 (2019)

Author Index

Printed in the United States
By Bookmasters